half-scratch •
magic

half-scratch •
magic

200 ways to pull dinner

out of a hat using a can of soup

or other tasty shortcuts

A Cookbook by James Beard Award–Winning Authors

Linda West Eckhardt & Katherine West DeFoyd

Clarkson Potter/Publishers
New York

Published by Clarkson Potter/Publishers, New York, New York.
Member of the Crown Publishing Group, a division of Random House, Inc.
www.randomhouse.com

CLARKSON N. POTTER is a trademark and POTTER and colophon are registered trademarks of Random House, Inc.

Printed in the United States of America

Design by Jan Derevjanik

Library of Congress Cataloging-in-Publication Data

Eckhardt, Linda West.
Half-scratch magic : 200 ways to pull dinner out of a hat using a can of soup or other tasty shortcuts / Linda West Eckhardt and Katherine West DeFoyd.—
1st ed. Includes index.
1. Quick and easy cookery.   I. DeFoyd, Katherine West.   II. Title.
TX833.5 .E29 2003
641.5'55—dc21   2002010408

ISBN 0-609-80851-6

10 9 8 7 6 5 4 3 2

First Edition

acknowledgments

Thanks to our editor, Pam Krauss, who saw the magic and pulled a few rabbits out of the hat herself. Ongoing gratitude to our agent, Susan Ginsburg, a true wizard. Kudos to Jennifer English of the Food and Wine Radio Network, who understood the illusion and gave us the signature recipe for the book—Chinese Tomato Soup—over the phone. Thanks to Joan Lebow, who helped shape and develop the metaphor with her charmed, wordsmith abilities. Thanks to Lizette Ryes, to whom we are grateful for her supernatural abilities with concept development and editing. Thanks to Diane DePaulis, who through a sleight of hand improved the book's design and helped us think through the disappearing cover art. Thanks to Kelly Volpe for her help stirring the cauldron and developing and testing recipes. Thanks to Jackie Herships, who helped us conjure up a public relations plan. Thanks to Patti Jo Lambert of Ketchum Communications and the Canned Food Alliance for their miraculous support. Thanks to Meredith Pollak for being such a charmed cook and entertainer. She and her mother, Peggy Vinyard, continue to inspire us to practice Louisiana Black Magic in the kitchen with pride. Finally, thanks to Gordon Murray, the chief warlock who works his magic every day in every way.

contents

introduction

Vanity Food should be the title of this book. Once upon a time, we cooked everything from scratch. We turned up our noses at frozen mashed potatoes, ready-made piecrusts, and fully cooked meat and poultry. Sometimes, as mother and daughter, we'd go to the grocery store together when we were working on a magazine article or new cookbook and needed ingredients to test. We remember feeling oh so smug when an onlooker gazed into the basket brimming with fresh vegetables, fish, and a few basics, saying, "Dinner is going to be good for you tonight." Yes, life was full of bottles of wine, weekly movie visits, novels, and lazy Sunday mornings to read the *Times.* Then boom . . . Katherine had twins. . . . Linda moved to New Jersey and took an e-commerce job. Life just got crazy.

Looking down into either of our grocery carts today you will see those frozen food items, chicken shortcuts, boxes of couscous and rice, even canned foods. To paraphrase the Talking Heads song, Katherine says she often finds herself muttering, "This is not my life, this is not my house, how did I get here?" Linda adds, "Amen."

Yet, in truth, frozen mashed potatoes, waffles, and canned beans often get both of us through the week. You know the regular sleight-of-hand breakfast, lunch, and dinner items. Because we write about food, our vanity is involved in all our food choices. Do we ever dare admit that we have actually determined the best sources for frozen stir-fry? No, never. We once heard our idol, Julia Child, say, "Never complain; never explain." And that is just what we do. When guests marvel that we can put such a sophisticated and delicious dinner on the table without breaking a sweat, we smile graciously and murmur "Oh, it's just something I threw together."

We never intended to live our lives running from one task to another on an ever-expanding mountain of demands. But it's a new millennium, and there you have it. Life has revved up until all of us are running as fast as we can.

Does this leave any time and space for cooking?

Some people have given up cooking altogether. Others have retreated behind a bunker of takeout boxes. But we still believe that the home-cooked meal may be the last bastion of civilization within the family and is something worth preserving. So we cook.

Setting the table, turning on the music, lighting the candles. Sitting down together at least once a day. These are important rituals within our family. We want to preserve them. (Well, okay—the candles, we light only in the dining room. For all those eat-in-kitchen suppers, we count it a success if everybody sits down together.)

We try to make cooking a pleasurable but easy thing to accomplish. For this book, our fourth as a mother-daughter cookbook writing team, we have tried to answer the question, Can half-scratch cooking be any good? Happily, we believe the answer is yes. We've come up with a number of memorable lunch, dinner, dessert, and potluck recipes that can fool even the biggest food snobs. The truth is that even the chefs we all admire (as seen on TV) use many tricks and convenience products to give us the sizzle as well as the steak, to enhance flavor in a hurry. If they can do it, why can't you?

We discovered there is a wealth of new products in the grocery store, and we tried most of them. We've found, for example, that marinara sauce is not only great for pasta, but has nearly a dozen other great uses. We've gone back to the future and explored the use of canned and jarred soups as a basis for main dishes and sauces.

We've blown out cake mixes into foundations for sensational desserts.

The big changes in the produce section have benefited us all. Salad in a bag, greens that are triple washed, baby carrots to pop in your mouth, sweet little grape tomatoes so succulent they hardly need any attention at all—these make it easier than ever to put something fresh, wholesome, and pretty on the plate. We've tried to find new and inventive ways to use these great products.

We admit it: As a culture, we're spoiled. Our standards have become absurdly high. We've eaten out too many times. Now we know the difference between a well-prepared and -presented meal and a careless one.

If we're going to cook at home, we want the results to look glorious, to taste heavenly—but not to result in hours in the kitchen, mountains of dirty dishes, or long nights to clean up. Nor do we want the expense of a steady diet of restaurant fare.

In other words, what we want are restaurant-quality meals without dining out and without working as hard as a chef and his backup crew do every night.

Is such a dream possible? Sure it is. We've hung out with chefs long enough to know they use a lot of taste-enhancing techniques and products. We've begged, borrowed, and stolen every good idea ever told us by chefs we've interviewed.

What is our goal? A gorgeous dinner we can have on the table in about a half hour. A short list of ingredients. Punched-up flavor that leaves them begging for more.

Can you do it? Of course you can. This book is designed for cooks at all skill levels. We've gone out of our way to not only tell you step-by-step what to do, but to also give you a synopsis of each step in case the phone rings, the baby screams, or you need to stop for a minute to answer the door.

We've divided the chapters according to magicians' secret ingredients. Got a pantry full of pasta and rice? Check out our chapter called "Thinking out of the Box." Only have time to pick up a roast chicken with company coming at six o'clock? Take a look at "Chicken: Off the Spit or Cooked and Carved." You'll find lots of good and fast answers to the nightly question of what's for dinner. Beginning with a cooked bird (or some of its parts) makes meals from upscale to down-home a matter of just minutes. Notice those fully cooked roasts, meatballs, and barbecue in the butcher case? We've found some terrific ways to make those products sing.

We have investigated the role the new generation of prepared foods can play in everyday cooking. A lot of food got fed to the dogs while we were testing for this book. It took tons of experimentation to come up with recipes that meet our exacting standards, and we're here to tell you that there are some prepared foods even the dogs wouldn't touch. At one point, we agreed the failure rate for recipe tests in this book was about one in two.

What we found in all our experimentation is that while manufacturers often get the basic product cooked just fine, their abilities to sauce and to finish sauces remain abysmal. The good news is that to whip up a little sauce on your own is usually quick and easy and makes it look as if you slaved all day. Often simply adding one fresh produce item can lift a bland dish to an entirely different level.

We didn't neglect those recurring domestic mysteries like what to do if friends call you from the corner and want to come on up for Sunday brunch—right now. Or how to throw a quick cocktail party when you have nothing on hand except the idea and the guest list.

The thing is, life is a party, an opportunity to celebrate, one day at a time. And we hope by using our book, you can feel like a child again, full of wonder, mouth agape because you not only pulled the rabbit out of the hat, but out of the oven as well, and it was as quick and satisfying as magic. We want to turn that ongoing mystery called life into a peaceful, happy moment.

Enjoy. Enjoy. Start at the dinner table.

what you'll find in this book

What on earth is half-scratch? Basically it means you let the food manufacturers do more than half the work. Think about it. It wasn't too long ago that if you wanted a chicken dinner, you had to cast an eye to the backyard chicken pen. But life has evolved. Yes, you can still buy live poultry if your city has a Chinatown or a Hispanic district, or if you live in the country, but only die-hard ethnic cooks and country families opt for a recipe that begins with wringing a chicken's neck.

The truth of it is, more and more of us have less and less time to devote to putting food on the table. First, we were satisfied to buy whole plucked chickens behind glass at a butcher's case. Then, about twenty years ago, the butchers began cutting up those chickens. Now, in the beginning of the twenty-first century, you can even buy that chicken cooked—and in several forms.

Yes. You can buy a whole roasted chicken, sometimes known as a rotisserie chicken, seen spinning beneath a flame in many a grocery store from coast to coast. You can also buy cooked and seasoned chicken parts in the refrigerated case at the grocery store. Actually, what you're buying is chicken breast that's been skinned, boned, and seasoned, then slow cooked to guarantee a tender product. All you do is rip open the package and compose your dinner using the fully cooked chicken, some flavor boosters and seasonings, and perhaps a package of salad greens.

That's half-scratch at its best.

Not that chicken is the only thing we can pull out of our hat at supper time. The beef people have weighed in and given us fully cooked pot roasts complete with gravy, cooked ground beef called ground beef crumbles, and even perfect slabs of rare prime rib.

And protein is only the beginning. Haven't you noticed the plethora of marinara sauces taking up more and more space in the canned vegetable aisle? Do you really believe the only thing you can do with a jar of marinara is dump it onto a steaming mountain of spaghetti? We don't think so. We've found a number of uses for marinara besides pasta-and-sauce suppers.

This brings us to one of our pet peeves. And that is people telling us "If you've seen one, you've seen 'em all." Not true. We have opened competing brands of a number of these products. No, we won't tell you what the horrid ones are, but we will tell you by brand name what we find acceptable, or in a few cases exceptional.

It's what we're here for. We've done your homework for you. We've cooked, and tasted and tried products until we found just exactly which barbecue sauce or spaghetti sauce or salad dressing we like.

Does this mean you will agree with us or even be able to find exactly what we did? Not necessarily. Does this mean you have to skip over recipes where we recommend a brand because you can't find it or don't like it? Get over it. You are a half-scratch magician yourself now. Make your own choices. It's your palate and your dinner table and your family you have to please. If you prefer spaghetti sauce with a healthy dose of sugar in its ingredient list, by all means use it. Just don't ask us to do so. The dishes you turn out will be different from the recipes we give that specify a branded product, but hey, that's the nature of recipe development. If you get a finished dish that makes you happy, that's what counts.

And for heaven's sake, if you see a recipe that calls for frozen shrimp and you will use only fresh, please, be our guest. In other words, all of us have lines we will not cross.

Never let the lack of an ingredient stop you from trying a recipe. When in doubt, substitute. The result you get will be different from the recipe as written, but who knows? It might even be better. Give it a shot.

Your half-scratch may never be the same as ours. You may be a whiz at making and freezing pesto from your garden to use all winter. If so, by all means whiz away. The rest of us are grateful that a commercial product that's acceptable is available in specialty markets and at Costco.

Let go and do what works for you.

We'd like to hear from you. If you have magic tricks up your sleeve, recipes that start with a processed food, send us a note via e-mail. We'll see to it that it's considered for our next volume of "half-scratch magic" dishes. We're interested in what enchants you. We like to baffle and amaze, and we know you do, too. Let us hear from you.

Send your kitchen tricks to leckhardt@mindspring.com or kdefoyd@mindspring.com.

Best regards, and happy sorcery.
Linda Eckhardt and Katherine DeFoyd
Masters of disguise—aka cooks

part one

fresh and frozen wizardry

Walk around the perimeter of your grocery store these days, and you'll find everything you need to make dinnertime magic: rotisserie chicken and sliced meat in the deli section; cooked and carved chicken parts, fully cooked roasts, and ground beef crumbles in the meat case; pizza crusts, prepared polenta, and fresh pasta in the dairy case; and a world of healthy choices in the produce section. Even the freezer case yields some great half-scratch staples. Best of all, with a touch of your wand and a minimal investment of time (promise!) each and every one of these items can be transformed into something you can serve with pride and say, "I made it myself."

chapter one ⋆ protein power

Rotisserie chicken has saved many a family from yet another night at the drive-through window, but let's face it—you're unlikely to win much applause the umpteenth time you plop a basic bird on the table. Use the recipes that follow to make that bird soar . . . and give new zest to other timesaving main-course standbys like cooked pot roasts and meatballs, sliced deli meats, and more. They're so savory that if you didn't know better, even *you* would think you had spent hours in the kitchen rather than minutes at the market. And we won't tell if you don't. . . .

deli voodoo

The deli is no longer limited to pastrami and roast beef. Today, you see mashed potatoes, pasta salads napped with vinaigrettes, quesadillas, cooked chicken and veal cutlets—even poached salmon. The sheer sorcery of mixing and matching a few ready-to-eat choices into a new dinner item may seem as wondrous as watching a woman in a box being sawed in half by a magician—only to rise at the end to great applause. With these recipes, get ready to take your bow.

1. **Roast Beef Sandwiches with Arugula and Wasabi Spread**

2. **Shaman Southwestern Roast Beef Salad on Top of Corn Salsa**

3. **Vietnamese Roast Beef Salad**

4. **Ham and Mango Chutney Sandwiches**

5. **Madras Turkey Quesadillas**

6. **Smoked Turkey, Cream Cheese, and Cranberry Sauce Sandwiches**

7. **Smoked Turkey, Mango Chutney, and Blue Cheese Sandwiches**

8. **Smoked Turkey and Baked Eggs with Wild Mushrooms and Spinach**

9. **Smoked Salmon Spinach Napoleons**

10. **Gingered Salmon on a Bed of Slaw**

11. **Provençal Spinach and Goat Cheese Wraps**

roast beef sandwiches with arugula and wasabi spread

Thinly sliced roast beef is easy to find and much improved with wasabi, a dry magical powder (just add water). It also complements the peppery arugula.

1 tablespoon dried wasabi powder

½ cup mayonnaise

4 crusty Italian sandwich rolls, split

1 pound thinly sliced roast beef (preferably fresh cut from the deli section of a better grocery store)

Salt and freshly milled pepper

1 bunch arugula

makes 4 servings
time: 10 minutes

1 Hydrate the wasabi.
In a small bowl, stir together the wasabi and 1 tablespoon of water.

2 Make the spread.
In another small bowl, stir together the mayonnaise and the wasabi.

3 Make the sandwiches.
Spread the rolls with the wasabi mayonnaise. Layer on the roast beef, and season with salt and pepper to taste. Top with the arugula, and serve.

tip: Wasabi powder is a classic ingredient that we keep on hand at all times. It will last a long time and can be used to spice up many sauces. Try stirring just a little into sour cream or heavy cream for an instant wasabi cream sauce that's great on top of fish or chicken.

shaman southwestern roast beef salad on top of corn salsa

The earthy flavor of roast beef works well with the smoky flavor of chipotle and the sweet flavor of corn. And of course, it is all great on top of plain old cold, juicy iceberg lettuce on a hot day.

makes 4 servings
time: 15 minutes

- ¼ cup fresh lime juice
- ½ cup chopped cilantro
- 2 teaspoons chopped canned chipotle in adobo or jalapeño pepper
- 1 garlic clove, finely chopped
- ½ cup olive oil
- ¾ pound thinly sliced roast beef, cut into thin strips
- 2 cups frozen corn kernels
- 1 large or 2 medium tomatoes, halved, seeded, and cubed
- 2 stalks celery, chopped
- ½ medium red onion, finely chopped
- ½ to ¾ head of iceberg or Boston lettuce, cut into thin strips
- 2 mangos, peeled, pitted and thinly sliced

1 Make the dressing.
In a medium bowl, stir together the lime juice, ¼ cup of the cilantro, the pepper, garlic, and olive oil.

2 Marinate the beef.
Toss the roast beef strips with half of the dressing to thoroughly coat each strip. Marinate the beef for at least 5 minutes.

3 Make the salsa.
In another medium bowl, toss together the corn, tomato, celery, red onion, and the remaining cilantro. Drizzle the salsa with the remaining dressing.

4 Arrange the salads.
Divide the lettuce among 4 plates, placing it in the center of each plate. Spoon some salsa onto the lettuce, and top with the marinated beef. Surround the mounds of salad with the mango slices. Serve at once.

vietnamese roast beef salad

Nuoc mam gives this all-in-one salad meal a complex flavor profile often associated with hours of cooking. Grab a package of shredded carrots, and you won't even resent having to chiffonade the greens.

makes 4 to 6 servings
time: 15 minutes

- 2 tablespoons peanut oil
- 2 garlic cloves, finely chopped
- 3 teaspoons Vietnamese fish sauce (*nuoc mam*)
- Juice of 1 lime (⅓ cup)
- 1½ teaspoons sugar
- ½ teaspoon hot red pepper flakes
- 1 pound thinly sliced roast beef, cut into ½-inch strips
- 1 head Boston or Bibb lettuce leaves, cut into thin strips*
- ½ cup fresh basil leaves, cut into thin strips
- ¼ cup fresh mint, cut into thin strips
- 1 cup shredded or grated carrot

1 Make the marinade.

In a large bowl, stir together the oil and garlic, and cook them in the microwave on HIGH (100 percent power) for 1 minute. Add the fish sauce, lime juice, sugar, and red pepper, and combine.

2 Marinate the roast beef.

Toss in the roast beef and let it sit in the marinade for 15 minutes.

3 Toss the greens.

In a large bowl, combine the lettuce, basil, and mint.

4 Compose the salad.

Arrange some of the greens on each plate and sprinkle with the carrots. Lift the meat from the marinade, and arrange it on the greens.

* Leafy greens cut into thin strips are called chiffonade. It's easy. Stack leaves with the stem ends together; then roll up the greens like a fat cigar. Use a chef's knife, and rock it back and forth horizontally across that "cigar" to make a neat pile of thinly sliced greens.

ham and mango chutney
sandwiches

Major Grey's chutney—keep it in your pantry for those days when your palate is in a panic for something flavorful. Here we use it on a sandwich, but the sky's the limit on this product.

1 baguette, cut in half lengthwise

½ pound thinly sliced deli ham

1 (8-ounce) jar mango chutney

makes 6 sandwiches
time: 5 minutes

Make the sandwiches.

Spread the chutney on both sides of the bread, layer the ham on top, and put the halves together. Cut the baguette into 6 sandwiches. Wrap the sandwiches in plastic wrap, and chill them until serving time.

madras turkey quesadillas

Pears and turkey are great together. Try a jar of select pears from the refrigerated case if the market has only rock-hard pears. If you have time, pick your fresh pears and let them ripen in a brown paper bag for two days for perfection.

8 tortillas, preferably toasted sesame flavor

¼ cup Curry Mayonnaise (page 182)

¾ pound smoked turkey breast, thinly sliced

2 firm, ripe Anjou pears, peeled, cored, and thinly sliced, lengthwise

½ pound shredded aged Gouda cheese

4 teaspoons butter

makes 4 servings
time: 20 minutes

1 Assemble the quesadillas.

Lay 4 of the tortillas on a work surface. Spread each tortilla with 1 tablespoon of Curry Mayonnaise. Top with the turkey and pear slices. Sprinkle shredded cheese over each, and top with a second tortilla. The quesadillas may be prepared up to this point and refrigerated for up to 2 hours.

2 Grill the quesadillas.

Heat a large skillet or griddle over medium-high heat. For each quesadilla, and cooking 1 at a time, add 1 teaspoon of butter to the pan. Fry the quesadilla until it is lightly browned and the cheese is melted, about 2 minutes per side. Cut each into quarters, and serve warm.

smoked turkey, cream cheese, and cranberry sauce sandwiches

Turkey with cranberries is a classic combination that has a way of surprising people "off season." For a fast meal, try this winner of a sandwich.

1 baguette, cut in half lengthwise

½ pound cream cheese

1 (15-ounce) can whole-berry cranberry sauce

½ pound smoked turkey, thinly sliced

makes 6 sandwiches
time: 10 minutes

Make the sandwiches.

Smear one side of the bread with cream cheese and one side with cranberry sauce. Layer the smoked turkey onto a baguette half, and top with the remaining half. Cut the baguette into 6 pieces. Wrap the sandwiches in plastic wrap, and chill them for up to 1 hour, or until serving time.

smoked turkey, mango chutney, and blue cheese sandwiches

Pick up almost all these ingredients in the deli section of your grocery store. Mango chutney works its magic again. Its complex flavor can tune up many old standards.

6 ounces mild blue cheese (such as Maytag, Gorgonzola, or Stilton)

1/4 cup plus 2 tablespoons mayonnaise

3 tablespoons bottled mango chutney, large pieces of mango chopped up

2 tablespoons chopped fresh parsley

Juice of 1/2 lemon

4 (5-inch) pieces Italian or French bread, cut in half lengthwise

1 pound thinly sliced smoked turkey

8 to 10 arugula or lettuce leaves

makes 4 sandwiches
time: 10 minutes

1 Make the cheese spread.

Mash together the cheese, mayonnaise, chutney, parsley, and lemon juice. Adjust the seasonings to your taste.

2 Make the sandwiches.

Spread the cheese mixture on each half of the bread slices. Layer each sandwich with turkey and lettuce. Serve as open-faced sandwiches or top with a second slice of bread.

smoked turkey and baked eggs with wild mushrooms and spinach

Is it a brunch dish or a perfect Sunday supper? You decide. One of our best discoveries in writing this book has been frozen mushrooms, which add that earthy exotic flavor and can always be kept around. If your guests are on their way, you can whip this together in minutes. Fabulous.

2 tablespoons olive oil

1 garlic clove, chopped

1½ cups frozen wild mushrooms (10-ounce box)

1 (10-ounce) package frozen creamed spinach

1 pound thinly sliced smoked turkey

4 large eggs

½ cup grated Parmesan cheese (2-ounce chunk)

makes 4 servings
time: 25 minutes

1 Preheat the oven to 400° F.

2 Make the base.
Combine the olive oil, garlic, and wild mushrooms in an 8 × 8 × 2-inch glass square baking dish. Microwave on HIGH (100 percent power) for 4 minutes. Add the frozen creamed spinach, and cook in the microwave for 4 more minutes, stirring once halfway through.

3 Build the dish.
Layer the turkey over the spinach mixture, and carefully crack the eggs on top, leaving them sunny-side up. Sprinkle the eggs with the Parmesan. Bake until the eggs are just set, 10 to 12 minutes. Serve warm with toast.

smoked salmon spinach napoleons

Okay, so we know napoleons are traditionally made with layers of puff pastry and crème anglaise, but regardless, layered foods are festive. These gorgeous pink-and-green savories are just the ticket when friends show up unexpectedly. Add a glass of chilled bubbly, and it's a party. We prefer dressing that's thin, rather than the wallpaper-thick gloppy stuff. If that's all you have, thin it with a little milk, and add a pinch of sugar.

1 (12-ounce) package triple-washed baby spinach	makes 4 servings
4 to 6 tablespoons ranch dressing	time: 10 minutes
¼ pound smoked salmon, thinly sliced	
8 bacon strips (crisp cooked or ready-cooked), crumbled	
1 red onion, thinly sliced	
Capers, for garnish	

1 Make the salad.
Toss spinach with just enough dressing to moisten it.

2 Make the napoleons.
Lay a salmon slice on each of 4 cold plates. Add a few leaves of dressed spinach and a slice of onion, and sprinkle with some crumbled bacon. Make another layer of salmon, spinach, onion, and bacon, and finish with a third slice of salmon. Serve the napoleons cold, garnished with capers.

gingered salmon
on a bed of slaw

This has become a summer night "pull the rabbit out of the hat" standby for those times when we just can't stand the heat in the kitchen. Many supermarkets now offer what is sometimes called "health salad," coleslaw dressed with vinaigrette rather than with mayonnaise. If you can't find it, buy traditional slaw and add a teaspoon of white wine or rice wine vinegar.

1 pint coleslaw

4 cold poached or grilled salmon fillets or steaks, from the deli section

$\frac{1}{2}$ cup Japanese-style ginger dressing

makes 4 servings
time: 5 minutes

Assemble the plates.

Mound equal servings of the coleslaw on 4 plates. Rest the salmon on top, and drizzle with the ginger dressing. Eat up.

provençal spinach and goat cheese wraps

Colorful spinach and puckery goat cheese wrapped up in a sophisticated roll; these are as easy to eat as they are to make.

½ pound fresh baby spinach	makes 2 servings
2 (8-inch) spinach tortillas	time: 10 minutes
¼ cup prepared olive tapenade	
6 ounces herbed goat cheese, crumbled into small pieces	
1 small tomato, thinly sliced	

1 Cook the spinach.

Clean the spinach leaves, discarding their stems. Place the leaves in a colander, and rinse well with cool water. Place the spinach in a small saucepan, and cook, covered, over medium-high heat just until it is wilted, 2 to 3 minutes. Remove from the heat.

2 Assemble the wraps.

Lay the tortillas on a flat work surface or plate, and spread them with the tapenade. Lay the cooked spinach leaves over the tapenade; then top with the goat cheese and tomato slices. Roll the tortillas up tightly, and place them, seam-side down, on serving plates. The wraps may be prepared up to 2 hours ahead of time and refrigerated. Serve the wraps at room temperature.

chicken: off the spit or cooked and carved

You'll see chicken turning on a spit in most any grocery store in America today. Do not just blindly rush in and think that all chickens are created equal. Be picky. Find a market that roasts its own birds, sells them right off the spit, and does not gum them up with chemical-laden dry rub. Do not even think about those you may see encased in plastic that have been suffering under a hot light for hours. The results will not be pretty.

The same is true for cooked chicken parts, which take up an ever-growing space in the meat case. Pick and choose among the products and brands. We like Perdue Short Cuts, which are cooked, carved breast meat. Some other brands, which shall herein go nameless, we wouldn't feed to the dog.

You must exercise the same discrimination when buying cooked products that you would when buying raw ingredients. You wouldn't equate some greasy spoon with a four-star restaurant, now, would you? That seems obvious. The same differences exist in cooked chickens.

It all comes down to paying attention to what you put into your mouth. Be prudent. Pick foods that are fresh, well prepared, and good for you. You'll be rewarded with a finished dish that looks and tastes as if you invested hours, not minutes.

rotisserie and roast chicken illusions

1. Cold Roast Chicken with Saffron Sauce

2. Honey Bourbon Black Magic Chicken on Spiced Sweet Potatoes

3. Orange-Glazed Chicken on a Bed of Citrus and Red Onion Chutney

4. Chicken with Apricot and Rosemary Glaze on White Beans

5. Rotisserie Chicken Tostada with Orange Aïoli

6. Three-Cheese Chicken Florentine Casserole

7. Currant and Citrus-Glazed Roast Chicken

cranberry sauce trickery: five mind-boggling cranberry sauce sides for rotisserie chicken

- Double-Ginger Cranberry Sauce

- Clove-and-Honey-Scented Cranberry Sauce

- Marsala-Cranberry Sauce with Cherries and Rosemary

- Cardamom–Five-Spice Powder Cranberry Sauce

- Cranberry and Horseradish Sauce

precarved chicken tricks

1. Chicken Enchiladas Veracruz

2. Ginger Cranberry Chicken Salad

3. Fast Mole Chicken Chili

4. Barbecue Chicken with Fresh
   Summer Fruits

5. Sesame Cilantro Chicken Salad

6. California Spinach Chicken Salad
   with Pecans

7. Thai Chicken Coconut Soup

8. Mustard Chicken in a Hurry

9. Calypso Chicken Pita

10. Welsh Rabbit out of the Hat

cold roast chicken with saffron sauce

On a hot day, stir lemon juice and saffron into mayonnaise to transform it into a special sauce. Only magic stardust might make this sauce even better. Serve it over a hot or cold chicken.

7 garlic cloves, halved

Juice of ½ lemon (2 teaspoons)

¼ teaspoon saffron threads

½ teaspoon salt

¼ teaspoon cayenne

1 cup mayonnaise

1 rotisserie chicken, quartered

makes 4 servings
time: 10 minutes

1 Cook the garlic.
Place the garlic cloves in a medium glass or ceramic bowl with ½ cup of water, and microwave on HIGH (100 percent power) for 4 minutes.

2 Purée the sauce.
Drain the garlic cloves, and combine them in a food processor or blender with the lemon juice, saffron threads, salt, cayenne, and mayonnaise. Purée until the mixture is smooth.

3 Serve the chicken.
Drizzle about 2 tablespoons of the sauce onto the bottom of each dinner plate. Arrange the chicken quarters to the side of the sauce, and serve, passing the remaining sauce separately.

honey bourbon black
magic chicken on spiced sweet potatoes

Honey, bourbon, and sweet potatoes—how can you lose with that flavor combo? Add a can of Glory Foods brand collard greens and glass of iced tea, and you can start to imagine yourself in Mississippi.

2 tablespoons honey

¼ cup bourbon whiskey

¼ teaspoon nutmeg

¼ teaspoon ground cloves

¼ teaspoon salt

2 tablespoons butter

1 rotisserie chicken, cut into serving pieces, any juices reserved

2 (16-ounce) cans sweet potatoes or yams, drained

½ cup raisins

½ cup chopped pecans or walnuts (for garnish)

makes 4 servings
time: 20 minutes

1 Preheat the oven to 400° F.

2 Make the glaze.
In a medium microwavable bowl, stir together the honey, bourbon, nutmeg, cloves, salt, and any juices that accumulated under the chicken. Microwave on HIGH (100 percent power) for 1 minute.

3 Assemble the casserole.
Butter a 13 × 9 × 2-inch baking dish generously. Place the chicken pieces, yams, and raisins in the baking dish, and drizzle them with the glaze. Bake for 15 minutes, basting the chicken with excess glaze after 7 minutes.

4 Finish the dish.
Garnish with the nuts, adjust the seasonings, and serve at once.

orange-glazed chicken on a bed of citrus and red onion chutney

On nights when you can't face one more bland meal, try this red onion and citrus sidekick. The chutney makes the chicken do a vanishing act.

4 tablespoons ($\frac{1}{2}$ stick) butter

$\frac{1}{4}$ cup orange juice

Juice and zest of 1 lime

1 rotisserie chicken, cut up into serving pieces

makes 4 servings
time: 20 minutes

Red Onion Chutney

1 large red onion, coarsely chopped

2 tablespoons extra-virgin olive oil

1 tablespoon sugar

3 tablespoons red wine vinegar

1 tablespoon orange juice

$\frac{1}{4}$ teaspoon salt

Freshly milled pepper

2 tablespoons minced cilantro (for garnish)

1 Preheat the oven to 400° F.

2 Make the glaze.
In a medium microwavable bowl, combine 2 tablespoons of the butter, the orange juice, and the lime juice. Microwave on HIGH (100 percent power) for 1 minute.

3 Glaze the chicken.
Butter a 13 × 9 × 2-inch baking dish generously. Place the chicken pieces in the baking dish, and drizzle them with the glaze. Bake for 10 minutes.

4 Make the chutney.

While the chicken reheats, combine the onion and olive oil in a medium-size glass bowl, and microwave on HIGH for 5 minutes. Stir in the sugar, red wine vinegar, orange juice, and salt, and cook on HIGH for 5 more minutes.

5 Finish the dish.

Remove the chicken from the oven, and spoon the chutney around the chicken pieces. Return the chicken to the oven, and cook for 5 more minutes. Sprinkle with black pepper and cilantro, and serve at once.

chicken with apricot and rosemary glaze on white beans

Apricot jam with a pinch of rosemary makes a great base. Sitting atop a bed of white beans, this dinner is great for friends, as well. Fresh rosemary will last up to three weeks in the refrigerator and you should always have white beans on the shelf.

¾ cup apricot jam

¼ cup packed brown sugar

1 tablespoon fresh rosemary needles (plus several sprigs for garnish)

1 rotisserie chicken, quartered

2 (15-ounce) cans white cannellini beans

Freshly milled pepper, to taste

makes 4 or more servings
time: 20 minutes

1 Preheat the oven to 350° F.

2 Make the glaze.
In the bowl of a food processor, combine the apricot jam, brown sugar, and rosemary needles and purée until smooth. Transfer the glaze to a microwavable bowl, and microwave on HIGH (100 percent power) for 1 minute.

3 Glaze the chicken.
In a large ovenproof Dutch oven, arrange the chicken on top of the white beans, and spoon or brush the chicken with the glaze. Season with the black pepper. Place the pot in the oven to reheat for 15 minutes. Garnish the chicken with rosemary sprigs, and serve hot or at room temperature.

rotisserie chicken tostada with orange aïoli

Here's a "give 'em the sizzle" lunch on a plate that belies the simplicity of its ingredients. There's no cooking whatsoever, just a composition of orange mango slices alternating with carved chicken breast layered between yellow corn tostada shells, with a mini-mountain of savory yellow-green butter lettuce and a sprinkle of bright green jalapeño bits atop the final shell—all stacked on a plate in an artful way that makes it look like a lunch served in a fine New York restaurant, which is where the idea originated.

¼ cup mayonnaise

2 garlic cloves, minced or pressed

1 teaspoon chili powder

2 tablespoons fresh orange juice

1 fully cooked chicken breast (about 11 ounces), carved into neat slices

1 head butter lettuce, washed, spun dry, and torn into bite-size pieces

6 tostada shells (flat crispy corn tortillas)*

1 ripe mango, peeled and cut into neat slices

1 fresh jalapeño, seeded and minced

makes 2 servings
time: 15 minutes

1 Make the dressing.

In a small bowl, stir together the mayonnaise, garlic, chili powder, and orange juice. In a second bowl, add half the dressing to the chicken slices, and toss them gently to mix. In a large bowl, toss the remaining dressing with the lettuce.

2 Compose the salad.

Lay a tostada shell on each plate. Arrange the chicken slices in a spoke pattern on top, alternating with slices of mango. Top with a second tostada shell. Mound with lettuce; then top with a third tostada shell. Garnish with minced jalapeño, and serve at once.

* To make tostada shells yourself, heat 2 teaspoons of vegetable oil in a heavy skillet over high heat. Add a 6-inch corn tortilla to the skillet, and fry it until crisp and browned on one side. Turn and cook the second side briefly; then drain the tortilla on paper towels. Add more oil to the skillet as you fry additional tortillas.

three-cheese chicken florentine casserole

Your basic comfort food gets a healthful update when made with bright fresh vegetables. Chop them in the food processor with five or six quick pulses per veggie.

½ pound penne pasta

1 tablespoon extra-virgin olive oil

1 cup frozen chopped onion

1 orange bell pepper, chopped

½ pound cremini mushrooms, chopped

1 (10-ounce) package triple-washed baby spinach

1 tablespoon dried tarragon

1 teaspoon paprika

2 cups cooked chicken meat, skinned, boned, in bite-size pieces

1 (10¾-ounce) can cream of chicken soup

1 cup grated Cheddar cheese (¼-pound chunk)

2 cups cottage cheese

½ cup freshly grated Parmesan cheese (2-ounce chunk)

makes 8 servings
time: 30 minutes

1 Cook the pasta.
In a large pot, bring 4 quarts of water to a boil. Add salt; then cook the penne according to package directions, about 8 minutes. Drain.

2 Cook the vegetables.
Meanwhile, in a large skillet, heat the oil over medium heat. Add the onion, bell pepper, and mushrooms to the skillet one at a time, stirring between each addition. Sauté for 3 minutes. Add the spinach, tarragon, and paprika, and cook until most of the liquid has evaporated, about 5 minutes.

3 Prepare the filling.
Stir together the chicken pieces with the soup and the cheeses.

4 Assemble and bake the dish.
Heat the oven to 350°F. Spritz a 9 × 13-inch glass baking dish with olive oil cooking spray. Layer in the drained penne, then the sautéed vegetables and the chicken-cheese mixture. Bake until the casserole is bubbly and brown, about 45 minutes. Cool on a rack. Cut into squares to serve.

currant and citrus-glazed roast chicken

Red currant jelly is a great base for so many sauces, and a long-known chef's trick for getting sweet and tart flavor notes into almost anything—even a rotisserie chicken. Keep it on hand.

½ yellow onion, finely chopped

2 tablespoons olive oil

1 tablespoon orange zest

1 teaspoon lemon zest

½ cup orange juice

½ cup red currant, plum, or other red seedless jelly

4 tablespoons (½ stick) butter

1 rotisserie chicken, cut into quarters

makes 4 servings
time: 30 minutes

1 **Preheat the oven to 400° F.**

2 **Make the sauce.**
In a large skillet over medium heat, sauté the onion in the olive oil. Cook until the onion becomes translucent, about 5 minutes. Stir in the orange zest, lemon zest, orange juice, and jelly, stirring and scraping up all the brown bits from the bottom of the skillet to deglaze the pan. Stir in the butter.

3 **Heat the chicken.**
Arrange the chicken pieces in a baking dish. Drizzle the chicken with the glaze. Heat for 10 minutes, and serve over yellow rice or couscous.

cranberry sauce trickery

The tart flavor of cranberry sauce has been the salvation of many a Thanksgiving table, bringing up what is otherwise a big bland bird. It works the same magic on smaller birds, too. The whole-berry variety now available in a can is a wonderful base for a sauce to improve many dinners. So wonderful is this little red jewel that we serve it with chops, store-bought rotisserie chicken, and deli sandwiches. These sauces can be made in advance and frozen. Not one takes more than fifteen minutes to put together, and all can transform a meal. Each recipe makes ten servings.

double-ginger
cranberry sauce

This sauce will leave your mouth tingling with its spicy ginger flavor. Use a blender or food processor to chop up the ginger. This sauce not only zips up a rotisserie chicken, but it also makes a good bed for shrimp sautéed in butter.

1 (16-ounce) can whole-berry cranberry sauce

1 tablespoon orange zest

¼ cup crystallized ginger, minced

½ teaspoon ground ginger

¼ teaspoon salt

Make the sauce.

In a medium glass bowl, stir together all the ingredients. Microwave on HIGH (100 percent power) for 4 minutes. Stir, and heat on HIGH for 4 more minutes, or until the sauce boils. Serve warm or at room temperature with chicken or shrimp.

clove-and-honey-scented
cranberry sauce

Peppery cloves, sour cranberries, and the distinct flavor of honey combine nicely to lend a hint of the Middle East to all-American cranberries. Try this sauce with rotisserie chicken, ham, or even an oily fish such as grilled Chilean sea bass. You won't be disappointed.

1 (16-ounce) can whole-berry cranberry sauce

½ cup honey

¼ teaspoon ground cinnamon

1 tablespoon grated orange zest

¼ teaspoon ground cloves

¼ teaspoon salt

1 bay leaf

Make the sauce.

In a medium glass bowl, stir together all the ingredients. Microwave on HIGH (100 percent power) for 4 minutes. Stir and heat on HIGH for 4 more minutes, or until the sauce boils. Serve warm or at room temperature alongside chicken, ham, or fish.

marsala-cranberry sauce with cherries and rosemary

Who knew that this classic Italian wine would marry so nicely with an American classic, the cranberry? Terrific with fowl or pork and a fruity glass of Burgundy.

1 (16-ounce) can whole-berry cranberry sauce

½ cup dry marsala

½ cup dried cherries

1 (12-ounce) bag frozen sour pie cherries

1 teaspoon brown sugar

½ teaspoon minced fresh rosemary

½ teaspoon ground allspice

¼ teaspoon salt

Make the sauce.

In a medium glass bowl, stir together all the ingredients. Microwave on HIGH (100% power) for 4 minutes. Stir and heat on HIGH for 4 more minutes, or until the sauce boils. Serve warm or at room temperature alongside a rotisserie chicken or roast pork.

cardamom–five-spice
powder cranberry sauce

The exotic flavors of cardamom and five-spice powder will delight you when combined with cranberry sauce.

1 (16-ounce) can whole-berry cranberry sauce

1 teaspoon cider vinegar

1 (16-ounce) can pears, drained and cut into small chunks

1 teaspoon ground cardamom

$\frac{1}{2}$ teaspoon five-spice powder

$\frac{1}{4}$ teaspoon salt

Make the sauce.

In a medium-size glass bowl, stir together all the ingredients. Microwave on HIGH (100% power) for 4 minutes. Stir and heat on HIGH for 4 more minutes, or until the sauce boils. Serve warm or at room temperature alongside chicken, turkey, or ham.

cranberry and horseradish sauce

Combining the sweet and sour flavors of cranberry sauce with the spicy hot flavor of horseradish makes for a real winner, and a lovely hot pink color.

1 (15-ounce) can whole-berry cranberry sauce

1 cup sour cream

2 tablespoons prepared white horseradish

Salt

Make the sauce.

In a medium glass bowl, stir together the cranberry sauce, sour cream, horseradish, and salt to taste until smooth. Microwave on HIGH (100 percent power) for 4 minutes. Stir and heat on HIGH for 4 more minutes, or until the sauce boils. Serve warm or at room temperature with rotisserie chicken, roast turkey, steak, or pork chops.

chicken enchiladas veracruz

For a Mexican dinner in a hurry, snatch up a package of cooked chicken breasts. Add a quick salad of iceberg wedges with a citrus vinaigrette. It's dinner and it's done.

12 (6-inch) corn tortillas

1 (11-ounce) package cooked carved chicken breast

2 cups shredded jalapeño Jack or Cheddar cheese

2 cups fresh salsa

2 cups sour cream

Sprigs of cilantro (for garnish)

makes 4 to 6 servings
time: 30 minutes or less

1 Prepare the tortillas.

Heat the oven to 375°F. Spritz a 9 × 13-inch baking dish with olive oil cooking spray. Heat the unopened package of tortillas in the microwave on HIGH (100 percent power) for about 20 seconds; then stack them in the prepared baking dish.

2 Make the enchiladas.

Arrange a row of chicken pieces down the middle of each tortilla. Add a pinch of grated cheese, and roll up the tortillas. Lay the rolled enchiladas in the baking dish, sides touching. Stir the salsa and sour cream together, and pour the mixture over the enchiladas. Top with the remaining cheese. Bake until the enchiladas are bubbly and hot, about 15 minutes.

3 Serve.

Arrange two or three enchiladas on heated plates. Garnish with cilantro sprigs.

ginger cranberry
chicken salad

Unlike their fresh counterparts, dried cranberries, sometimes called craisins, are available year-round. They, along with spicy ginger, give the concept of chicken salad new meaning.

¼ cup mayonnaise

1 teaspoon prepared horseradish

2 tablespoons Dijon mustard

1 orange, sectioned, seeded, and cut into chunks

1 cup dried cranberries (about 3 ounces)

1 tablespoon chopped fresh ginger

1 teaspoon chopped crystallized ginger

Juice and zest of ½ lemon

1 teaspoon sugar

2 (11-ounce) packages cooked carved chicken breast

1 stalk celery, finely chopped

1 firm apple, cored and chopped

½ cup chopped walnuts

1½ heads romaine lettuce or 1 bag Roman lettuce blend

makes 6 to 8 servings
time: 20 minutes

1 Make the dressing.
In the bowl of a food processor, combine the mayonnaise, horseradish, Dijon mustard, orange sections, cranberries, ginger, crystallized ginger, lemon juice, zest, and sugar. Pulse to mix into a rough purée.

2 Make the salad.
In a mixing bowl, toss together the chicken, celery, apple, and walnuts. Stir in the dressing, mixing thoroughly.

3 Assemble the plates.
Divide the greens among the plates, and top them with the chicken-cranberry salad. Serve at once.

fast mole chicken chili

This recipe makes a big batch of chili, but it keeps in the refrigerator up to a week and can be stored in the freezer against the day when a total code red means you have no time to cook. Either way, it tastes as if you cooked all day. Can't find dark, rich, sweet ancho chiles? Substitute a roasted red bell pepper and a jot of hot red pepper flakes. Adjust the heat with cayenne.

1 cup long-grain rice (3 cups cooked)

makes 10 to 12 servings
time: 30 minutes

Chili Paste

2 dried ancho chiles

¼ cup raw cashews or pine nuts

1 (15-ounce) can chicken broth

1 tablespoon olive oil

2 cups frozen chopped onion

6 garlic cloves, coarsely chopped

¼ cup raw cashews or pine nuts

2 tablespoons chili powder (Gebhardt's Eagle Brand is our favorite)

1 tablespoon ground cumin

⅛ teaspoon cayenne (optional)

1 teaspoon salt

¼ cup minced fresh cilantro leaves (plus additional, for garnish)

1 (14½-ounce) can fire-roasted diced tomatoes with juice (we like Muir Glen)

1 (15½-ounce) can black beans

1 (11-ounce) package cooked, carved chicken breast

1 ounce (1 square) unsweetened baking chocolate

Sour cream (for garnish)

Shredded *queso blanco* or other mild cheese (for garnish)

Prepared *pico de gallo* or salsa (for garnish)

Chopped cashews or pine nuts (for garnish)

1 Cook the rice.

In a saucepan, combine the rice with 2 cups of water. Raise to a boil over high heat; then cover, and reduce the heat to a bare simmer. Cook until the water is absorbed, about 15 minutes.

2 Make the chili paste.

In a small heavy skillet, heat the chiles just until toasty, a couple of minutes; then remove the seeds and stems. Place the chiles in a blender or food processor, and purée with the cashews and enough of the broth to make a thin paste.

3 Make the chili.

In a stewpot over medium heat, heat the oil and sauté the onion and garlic until translucent, about 3 minutes. Stir in the cashews, the chili powder, cumin, and cayenne. Add the salt, $1/4$ cup cilantro, tomatoes, beans, chicken, chocolate, the remaining broth, and the chili paste. Simmer for 5 minutes, stirring occasionally, until the chocolate melts and is incorporated.

4 Serve.

Spoon the cooked rice into bowls, add a serving of chili, and then top with sour cream, cheese, nuts, and cilantro, and a side of *pico de gallo*.

barbecue chicken with fresh summer fruits

This quick salad is fresh-tasting and too easy all at once. It will satisfy your craving for barbecued chicken without firing up the grill.

1 (11-ounce) package cooked, carved chicken breast

¼ cup prepared barbecue sauce*

1 (10-ounce) package mixed Mediterranean salad greens

1 pint fresh raspberries

1 cup cantaloupe or other melon pieces

¼ cup sliced almonds, toasted**

Raspberry vinaigrette or your favorite ranch salad dressing

makes 4 servings
time: 10 minutes

1 Season the chicken.

Combine the chicken and sauce, and heat them either in the microwave or on the stovetop to just under the boil.

2 Compose the salad.

Divide the greens among 4 salad plates. Fan out the chicken pieces atop the greens. Top with the berries and melon; sprinkle with the toasted almonds. Serve the dressing on the side.

* When we did a taste test trying ten barbecue sauces, K.C. Masterpiece was our hands-down favorite. If you have another favorite, by all means, use it.

** To toast almonds, arrange them one layer deep on the tray of a toaster oven or a baking sheet, and cook just until the nuts are fragrant, 2 to 3 minutes.

sesame cilantro
chicken salad

We buy cilantro every time we go to the grocery store, and so should you. It can perk up everyday meals, including scrambled eggs, a grilled cheese sandwich, and soups and salads. Store the cilantro bunch in the refrigerator in a cup full of water with a plastic-wrap bonnet to prevent desiccation of the leaves.

¼ cup sesame seeds

1 tablespoon sesame oil

1 tablespoon vegetable oil

Pinch of hot red pepper flakes

3 tablespoons rice wine vinegar

½ teaspoon sugar

1 (11-ounce package) cooked carved chicken breast

1 head butter or iceberg lettuce, cut into strips

1 cup chopped cilantro

2 scallions, chopped (for garnish)

2 tablespoons finely chopped crystallized ginger (optional)

makes 4 servings
time: 15 minutes

1 Make the dressing.
In the bottom of a large bowl, stir together 3 tablespoons of the sesame seeds, the sesame oil, vegetable oil, hot pepper flakes, vinegar, and sugar. Remove 2 tablespoons of dressing from the bowl, and reserve it for the greens.

2 Season the chicken.
Toss the chicken into the bowl with the remaining dressing, and mix well. Remove the chicken from the bowl, and set aside.

3 Dress the greens.
In the same bowl, toss the lettuce and cilantro with the reserved dressing, and mix them thoroughly.

4 Arrange the plates.
Divide the greens among 4 plates, and top with the chicken, chopped scallions, chopped ginger, and remaining sesame oil.

california spinach chicken salad with pecans

Toasting pecans takes only a minute but that flavor booster raises this salad to another level. Pick up a bottle of California's own invention, Catalina salad dressing, and before you know it, surf's up for a quick lunch.

1 (11-ounce) package cooked carved chicken breast

1 cup Catalina salad dressing

1 (10-ounce) package triple-washed baby spinach leaves

1 cup sliced strawberries

½ cup pecan halves, toasted*

makes 4 servings
time: 20 minutes

1 Prepare the chicken.
Toss the chicken with ½ cup of the salad dressing.

2 Compose the salads.
Divide the spinach among 4 salad plates. Top with the chicken, strawberries, and pecans. Serve the remaining salad dressing on the side.

* Quickly toast pecan halves in the toaster oven just until fragrant or on a baking sheet in a hot oven for 2 to 3 minutes. Take care not to burn them.

thai chicken coconut soup

Make magic with a package of chicken, a box and two cans! Serve alongside a salad with peanut dressing, and this pucker-your-lips soup will leave you satisfied.

1 (32-ounce) can chicken broth (4 cups)

1 (14-ounce) can unsweetened coconut milk

1 tablespoon sugar

1 tablespoon fish sauce (*nuoc mam*) or soy sauce

2 tablespoons finely julienned fresh ginger

Juice and zest of 1 large lime

1 cup water

1 (11-ounce) package cooked carved chicken breast

4 scallions, cut into 1-inch pieces

1 (15-ounce) can straw mushrooms, drained

¼ teaspoon hot red pepper flakes

¼ cup chopped cilantro

makes 4 servings
time: 15 minutes

1 Make the broth.

In a soup pot, combine the chicken broth, coconut milk, sugar, fish sauce, ginger, lime juice and zest, and water. Bring to a boil over high heat, then reduce the heat to a simmer, and cook for about 10 minutes.

2 Finish the soup.

Stir in the chicken, scallions, mushrooms, red pepper flakes (you may use less or more to taste), and cilantro. Bring to a boil, and cook for 3 to 5 minutes. Serve hot.

mustard chicken in a hurry

Often made with rabbit, this is classic French bistro fare. Here it's supper in minutes, instead of an hour. Serve it over rice or just with a baguette, et voilà!

2 tablespoons olive oil

1 medium yellow onion, thinly sliced

2 cups frozen wild mushrooms, thawed and sliced

1 (11-ounce) package cooked carved chicken breast

½ cup Dijon mustard, regular or grainy

1 cup dry white wine

½ cup chopped fresh parsley

makes 4 servings
time: 20 minutes

1 Sauté the onions and mushrooms.

In a 10- or 12-inch skillet over medium heat, heat the olive oil. Stir in the onions, and cook them for 4 to 5 minutes, or until they become translucent. Stir in the mushrooms, and cook for 4 to 5 minutes longer.

2 Finish the stew.

Stir in the chicken, mustard, and white wine. Reduce the heat to low, and simmer for 5 minutes. Just before serving, stir in all but 2 tablespoons of the parsley. Serve in a wide soup bowl over noodles or rice, or just with a baguette. Garnish with the remaining parsley.

calypso chicken pita

Pita breads make a wonderful, convenient base for individual pizzas, and can be topped with virtually anything you like. In this jerk-seasoned combo the spices of the Caribbean will take you to a place where life moves more slowly.

1 (11-ounce) package cooked carved chicken breast

⅓ cup Jamaican jerk marinade

2 onion pitas

1 ripe mango, peeled, pitted and thinly sliced

¼ cup thinly sliced Vidalia onion

½ small red bell pepper, finely diced

makes 4 servings
time: 20 minutes

1 Prepare the chicken.
In a large skillet, heat the chicken with ¼ cup of the jerk marinade over medium heat for 3 to 4 minutes.

2 Assemble the pizzas.
Lay the pitas on a work surface, and brush them with the remaining jerk marinade. Arrange the mango and onion slices on the pitas, and then mound the chicken over the top. Sprinkle with the diced red peppers. Cut each pita in half, and serve warm.

welsh rabbit out of the hat

Welsh rabbit, a Cheddar cheese sauce that was ubiquitous during the 1960s, is just like Raquel Welch—still great. Soup it up a bit, and it's a great accompaniment to chicken, poached eggs, vegetables, fish, noodles, or just toast. If chili powder isn't your thing, choose any of the alternate flavor boosters below.

1 (10-ounce) box frozen Stouffer's Welsh Rarebit Creamy Cheddar Cheese Sauce

1 tablespoon chili powder

1 (10-ounce) package cooked carved chicken breast

1 (10-ounce) box couscous

makes 4 servings
time: 10 minutes

1 Mix the sauce.
Cook the sauce in the microwave on HIGH (100 percent power) for 6 to 7 minutes. Stir in the chili powder or alternative seasoning. Heat chicken in the microwave for 1 minute.

2 Cook the couscous following package directions.

3 Assemble the dish.
Spoon the fluffed couscous onto 4 warm dinner plates. Top with cooked chicken pieces; then spoon the sauce over. Serve hot.

alternative seasonings:

¼ cup chopped scallions

1 teaspoon five-spice powder

1 tablespoon herbes de Provence

1 tablespoon horseradish

1 to 2 cloves garlic, finely chopped

½ red onion, finely chopped

¼ pint jar pimientos, finely chopped

2 tablespoons drained capers

2 tablespoons sweet pickle relish

frozen fish and shrimp

Making a special trip to the fish market does not jibe with the half-scratch philosophy of one-stop shopping—but the offerings in the fresh seafood departments of most supermarkets can be iffy. Fortunately, you can go "ice fishing" in the freezer case and find the makings of some downright elegant fare that's ready when you are. And no, we're not talking fish sticks here; frozen shrimp and mixed seafood (available at several of the large warehouse club and discount gourmet chains) are so fresh-tasting, you may say good-bye to your fishmonger forever.

1. **Crabcake Bruschetta**

2. **Shrimp Peanut Noodles**

3. **Spicy Shrimp on a Bed of Sautéed Baby Spinach**

4. **Galveston Fish Chowder**

5. **Provençal Seafood Stew**

crabcake bruschetta

These quick hors d'oeuvres can double as a meal, great for when people drop by unexpectedly.

¼	cup extra-virgin olive oil
2	garlic cloves, finely chopped
12	frozen crabcakes*
½	cup dry white wine
2	ripe tomatoes, halved, seeded, and diced
2 to 3	tablespoons chopped fresh parsley
½	baguette, sliced ½ inch thick, brushed with olive oil, and toasted

makes 4 servings
time: 10 minutes

1 Cook the crabcakes.

Coat the bottom of a heavy saucepan with the olive oil. Sauté the garlic until it just begins to turn golden, about 1 minute. Add the crabcakes, and cook over medium heat for about 8 minutes, until the cakes turn golden brown. Turn once.

2 Finish the topping.

Add the white wine, and cook, stirring constantly, for about 2 minutes, scraping up the browned bits from the bottom of the pan. Stir in the tomatoes and parsley, and cook for 2 minutes. Break up the crabcakes with a spoon.

3 Make the bruschettas.

Spoon 2 teaspoons of the crabcake topping onto each piece of toasted bread.

*To order Chesapeake Bay Gourmet crab cakes, call 1-800-432-2722 or visit www.cbgourmet.com.

shrimp peanut noodles

Got frozen shrimp and a jar of peanut butter? You've got the makings of a Thai classic. Use any dried pasta you can lay hands on and feel free to vary the veggies.

1 tablespoon salt

½ pound dried linguine (or other pasta)

1 tablespoon peanut oil

2 garlic cloves, smashed

2 teaspoons grated fresh ginger

1 pound frozen large peeled shrimp

1 red bell pepper, chopped

½ pound snow peas

1 carrot, shredded

½ cup chopped fresh cilantro (for garnish)

makes 4 servings
time: 20 minutes

Dressing

1 cup chicken broth

½ cup chunky peanut butter

3 tablespoons rice vinegar

1 teaspoon chili garlic sauce (such as Lee Kum Kee)

1 Cook the pasta.

In a big saucepot, bring 6 quarts of water to a boil. Add the salt, and break the linguine in half before dropping it in the water. (This makes serving easier.) Cook until al dente (about 8 minutes); drain well.

2 Sauté the vegetables and shrimp.

In a large skillet, heat the oil over high heat. Add the garlic and ginger, and sauté for about 30 seconds. Add the shrimp, and cook until it begins to brown on the edges; then toss in the bell pepper, pea pods, and carrot. Cook just until the pea pods begin to brown, about 2 minutes; then add the dressing ingredients. Stir well; then cook for about 5 minutes.

3 Combine and serve.

Add the drained pasta to the vegetables and shrimp. Toss well, and turn out onto warmed plates. Serve sprinkled with cilantro.

spicy shrimp on a bed of
sautéed baby spinach

Now that you can buy baby spinach in those triple-washed cellophane packs; frozen shrimp already cleaned, cooked, and peeled; and terrific punched-up flavors in Old Bay and Annie's seasonings, you have the basis for a fast and fabulous lunch. Sauté the shrimp first; then, in the same skillet, sauté the spinach. Baby spinach cooks up so fast, you dare not take your eye off the skillet.

1 pound frozen jumbo (16- to 20-count) peeled shrimp (we like Contessa)

½ cup plain yogurt

1 tablespoon Old Bay Seasoning

¼ cup plus 2 tablespoons olive oil

12 garlic cloves, chopped

½ medium red onion, thinly sliced

1 pound baby spinach

½ teaspoon sea salt

½ teaspoon cracked black pepper

1 tablespoon Annie's Naturals Sea Veggie & Sesame Vinaigrette (or sherry vinegar)

makes 4 servings
time: less than 20 minutes

1 Prepare the shrimp.

Add the shrimp to a bowl or large resealable plastic bag along with the yogurt and Old Bay. Seal the bag, and toss to mix well. Marinate for 10 to 15 minutes on the counter-top or up to 1 hour in the refrigerator.

2 Sauté the shrimp.

Coat a large skillet with half the olive oil. Lift the shrimp from the marinade with tongs, and cook just until they are pink and curled, turning only once, for 3 to 4 minutes. Transfer the cooked shrimp to a warm platter and cover.

3 Cook the vegetables.

Heat the same skillet over medium-high heat. Coat the skillet with the remaining oil, dredging up bits from the bottom; then add the garlic and onion. Cook and stir for about 45 seconds, and then add the spinach. Stir-fry until the spinach wilts, tossing with tongs. Season to taste with the salt and pepper. Finish with a tablespoon of Annie's vinaigrette or sherry vinegar. Divide among 4 dinner plates, and top with the shrimp, laid out in an artful circle. Serve at once.

galveston fish chowder

Next time you're at the supermarket, pick up a one-pound block of frozen fish—we used cod, but you could use perch or others. It's too easy. You don't even have to do more than half thaw the fish before you cut it into domino-size bites.

1 tablespoon olive oil

1 cup frozen chopped onion

1 stalk celery, minced

1 teaspoon chili powder

1 (15-ounce) can chopped Italian-style tomatoes and juice

1½ cups fresh or frozen corn kernels

½ teaspoon salt

1 teaspoon sugar

1 tablespoon Worcestershire sauce

1 pound fresh or frozen fillet of cod (or other firm-fleshed fish), cut into bite-size chunks

¼ cup minced fresh parsley

makes 4 servings
time: 20 minutes

1 Sauté the vegetables.

In a soup pot, heat the oil; then sauté the onion and celery with the chili powder until the onion is translucent, about 3 minutes. Add the tomatoes, corn, 2 cups of water, salt, sugar, and Worcestershire, and cook for 10 minutes.

2 Cook the fish in the soup.

Add the cod and cook until it's opaque, about 5 minutes. Stir in the parsley, and serve.

provençal seafood stew

People who live near the water know you can make a quick fish stew out of the day's catch—whatever that may be. We're likely to go fishing in our frozen compartment of the refrigerator. Shrimp freezes well, as do clams and squid. Use singly or in combination, as your freezer provides. And once you buy that clam broth—it comes in a bottle and is usually sold on the shelf at the market near the canned fish—you'll know you're on your way to quick and satisfying stew. Feel free to add or substitute fish and shellfish to this dish.

1 tablespoon olive oil

1 cup frozen chopped onion

1 celery stalk with leaves, chopped

2 garlic cloves, smashed

1 (16-ounce) can chopped tomatoes and juice

1 (15-ounce) can low-sodium chicken broth or clam broth

Salt and freshly milled pepper

$\frac{1}{4}$ teaspoon saffron

1 pound frozen peeled and deveined medium shrimp

12 small clams or mussels (or both) or $\frac{1}{2}$ pound frozen squid, clam meat, octopus (optional)

$\frac{1}{4}$ cup chopped fresh parsley

Juice and grated zest of 1 orange

makes 4 servings
time: 30 minutes or less

1 Sauté the vegetables.
In a stewpan, heat the oil. Add the chopped onion, celery, and garlic. Sauté the vegetables in the hot oil; then add the tomatoes and broth.

2 Make the soup.
Bring the mixture to a boil, seasoning with salt and pepper to taste, and the saffron. Simmer for 10 minutes; then add the shrimp and optional clams or other seafood. Cook until the shrimp turns pink and the clams and mussels open, 3 to 5 minutes.

3 Serve.
Stir in the parsley and orange juice and zest, and serve in wide-mouth soup bowls.

it's a grind: ground beef crumbles, ground meat, and cooked sausage

Ground meats are the traditional quick dinner in American kitchens, but who says you can't improve on a good thing? Now you can buy recipe-ready, fully cooked ground beef, known as ground beef crumbles, almost everywhere. If your supermarket doesn't have it yet, speak to the manager; once you try this handy product, you'll find it indispensable.

That said, you can certainly make any of the recipes in this section with regular ground beef; browning the meat in a skillet will add a scant ten minutes to the overall prep time. And if you can afford that extra ten minutes, try one of the recipes that uses one of the other ground meats you can buy these days, like turkey or lamb; you'll find them just as fast as good old hamburger meat and a welcome change.

Lastly, our hats off to cooked sausages. They come nicely spiced and add a smoky taste to quick soups and stews in a jiffy. They keep for weeks in the fridge and even longer in the freezer, so stock up.

1. **Beefy Taco Salad**

2. **Beef, Black Bean, and Salsa Burritos**

3. **Chili Beef Burgers in a Hurry**

4. **Mexican Corona Beef and Beer Soup in a Tortilla Bowl**

5. **Spicy Serrano Sonoran Beef Tacos with Currant Pico**

6. **North African Roll-ups**

7. **Great Salsa Verde Calzone**

8. **Ground Lamb and Tomato Cinnamon Sauce and Corn**

9. **Middle Eastern Salad with Lamb and Pita Triangles**

10. **Thirty-Minute Turkey Mole Stew**

beefy taco salad

You were wondering how the fast-food places manage to get those orders out so quickly? Precooked beef, preshredded lettuce and cheeses, and cheap help. Only you know what you're worth per hour, but precooked beef is worth its weight in gold. Only have raw ground beef? Just add ten minutes to brown it with the onions and spices.

2 tablespoons canola oil	makes 6 servings
1 cup chopped onion	time: 15 minutes

2 tablespoons canola oil

1 cup chopped onion

3 garlic cloves, smashed

1 tablespoon chili powder (we prefer Gebhardt's)

½ teaspoon ground cumin

¼ teaspoon cayenne

1 pound fully cooked ground beef crumbles

Salt and freshly milled pepper (to taste)

2 cups shredded iceberg lettuce (12-ounce package)

1 cup shredded Mexican cheese blend or shredded Cheddar cheese

¼ cup plus 2 tablespoons sour cream

1 teaspoon chopped cilantro

6 large black olives

1 Cook the seasonings.

In a large skillet over medium-high heat, heat the oil. Add the onion, garlic, chili powder, cumin, and cayenne, and sauté until the onion turns golden, about 2 minutes. Add the beef and salt and pepper to taste, and heat through.

2 Compose the salads.

Divide the lettuce among 6 dinner plates. Top with a scoop of cooked meat mixture. Top with cheese, sour cream, cilantro, and a black olive. Serve at once with a side of tortilla chips.

beef, black bean, and salsa burritos

Mondo burritos have fueled a generation of hungry kids. Here's one recipe they can make themselves.

1 cup chopped onions

4 garlic cloves, smashed

2 tablespoons canola oil

1 tablespoon chili powder (we prefer Gebhardt's)

$\frac{1}{2}$ teaspoon ground cumin

1 pound fully cooked ground beef crumbles

Salt and freshly milled pepper

1 (16-ounce) can black beans

4 (8-inch) flour tortillas

1 (12-ounce) package iceberg lettuce salad mix

1 cup prepared or fresh salsa

$\frac{1}{2}$ cup shredded Mexican cheese blend or Cheddar cheese

$\frac{1}{4}$ cup sour cream

$\frac{1}{4}$ cup chopped cilantro

1 fresh jalapeño, minced

makes 4 servings
time: 15 minutes

1 Season the beef.

In a large skillet, brown the onion and garlic in the oil over medium-high heat until golden, about 5 minutes. Add the chili powder, cumin, ground beef crumbles, and salt and pepper to taste. Stir to combine.

2 Prepare the components.

Meanwhile, in a medium pan, heat the beans to a boil, and then drain. Microwave the tortillas in the package they came in for about 15 seconds. Remove 4 and reserve the rest for another use. Store in the refrigerator.

3 Assemble the burritos.

Lay the tortillas on individual dinner plates. To each, add a portion of meat, beans, salad mix, salsa, cheese, sour cream, and cilantro. Fold the burrito like an envelope, folding in the sides first, then rolling to make a fat roll. Serve at once with minced jalapeño on the side.

chili beef burgers in a hurry

Don't tell anybody how easy this is. Just let them think of you as a chili queen.
Stock up on flavored tomatoes in cans. Not only do grocers sell chili-seasoned
tomatoes, but also Italian and Tex-Mex Robel tomatoes. All different, all delicious.

1 (15½-ounce) can chili beans
in chili sauce, drained

1 (14½-ounce) can chili-seasoned
chunky tomatoes, undrained

1 cup canned or frozen Mexican-style corn, drained

1 pound fully cooked beef crumbles

1 tablespoon chili powder (we prefer Gebhardt's)

Salt and freshly milled pepper

6 large hamburger buns

1 cup grated Cheddar cheese

¼ cup chopped cilantro

makes 6 servings
time: 15 minutes

1 Make the filling.
In a large saucepan, combine the beans, tomatoes, and corn. Heat to a boil. Add the cooked beef crumbles, chili powder, and salt and pepper to taste.

2 Assemble the burgers.
Heat the buns in a warm oven (about 225°F.), or in a toaster oven; then divide them among 6 dinner plates. Fill the bread with a scoop of meat mixture, sprinkle with cheese and cilantro, and serve at once.

mexican corona beef and beer soup in a tortilla bowl

You've seen those chalupa bowls made from tortillas in the Mexican section of the grocery store? Use them, and you won't even have a bowl to wash, only a plate to rinse. If your market sells Rotel-brand canned tomatoes, buy them. Otherwise search out a chile-tomato combo or use a small can of tomatoes plus two ounces of canned chopped chiles.

2 tablespoons canola oil

1 cup fresh or frozen chopped onion

4 garlic cloves, smashed

1 tablespoon chili powder (we prefer Gebhardt's)

1 teaspoon ground cumin

1/4 teaspoon cayenne

1 pound fully cooked beef crumbles

2 (10 1/2-ounce) cans beef consommé

1 (15 1/4-ounce) can Mexican-style corn, drained

1 (10-ounce) can diced tomatoes with green chiles, undrained

1 bottle pilsner-type beer, such as Corona

6 medium chalupa shells*

6 tablespoons sour cream

2 tablespoons chopped cilantro

makes 6 servings
time: 15 minutes

1 Season the beef.

In a medium soup pot, heat the oil. Brown the onion and garlic over medium heat until translucent, about 5 minutes, adding the chili powder, cumin, and cayenne near the end. Add the beef, and heat through.

2 Make the soup.

Add the consommé, corn, tomatoes with their juices, and beer. Cook for about 10 minutes.

3 Serve.

Arrange one chalupa shell on each dinner plate or inside a rimmed soup bowl. Spoon in a serving of soup, and top with sour cream and cilantro. Serve at once.

* Chalupa shells are easy to make, too. Press a flour tortilla into a 2-cup microwave-safe soup bowl. Microwave 3 bowls at a time on HIGH for about 5 minutes, or until tortillas are slightly crisp, rotating and rearranging the bowls twice. Or just serve the soup in bowls and pass the hot tortillas.

spicy serrano sonoran beef
tacos with currant pico

The Sonoran Desert runs from the northern part of Mexico up through California and Arizona. The sun is hot. The thirst is ever-present. Quick beef tacos beg for a beer. Go get 'em.

1 tablespoon canola oil

1 cup chopped onion

1 pound fully cooked beef crumbles

Salt and freshly milled pepper

makes 6 servings
time: 15 minutes

Currant Pico

1 cup currants (or raisins, dried cranberries, blueberries)

½ cup cilantro leaves

1 serrano chile, seeded

Juice and zest of 2 limes

6 crisp taco shells, warmed

¼ cup sour cream

Lime wedges (for garnish)

1 Make the filling.
In a large skillet, heat the oil. Sauté the onion over medium heat until it's translucent. Add the beef crumbles, and heat through, seasoning to taste with salt and pepper, about 5 minutes total.

2 Make the pico.
Add to a food processor bowl the currants, cilantro leaves, chile, and lime juice and zest. Pulse off and on until the mixture is finely chopped.

3 Assemble the tacos.
Stir half the pico into the beef mixture. Fill the taco shells with the beef; then top with the remaining pico. Finish with jot of sour cream. Serve with lime wedges on the side.

north african roll-ups

You may wonder what a recipe with such a long ingredient list is doing in a book like this. Trust us—just line up the spice jars on your counter, measure, and dump—it's three minutes of work that tastes like hours of simmered-in flavor.

2 tablespoons olive oil

½ cup chopped onion

1 tablespoon grated fresh ginger

2 garlic cloves, smashed

Juice and zest of ½ lemon

1 teaspoon soy sauce

1 teaspoon dry sherry

2 tablespoons chopped cilantro

1 teaspoon chili powder (we prefer Gebhardt's)

½ teaspoon ground cumin

½ teaspoon ground turmeric

¼ teaspoon dried marjoram

Pinch of saffron

1 teaspoon harissa or other hot sauce

1 pound fully cooked beef crumbles

Salt and freshly milled pepper

6 large flour tortillas, red or green, or North African flatbreads

makes 6 servings
time: 15 minutes

1 Make the filling.

In a large skillet, heat the oil over medium heat. Sauté the onion, ginger, and garlic until translucent, about 5 minutes. Add the lemon juice and zest, soy sauce, sherry, cilantro, chili powder, cumin, turmeric, marjoram, saffron, hot sauce, and beef crumbles, and mix well. Season with salt and pepper to taste, and heat through.

2 Fill the rollups.

Lay out a large flour tortilla, and spoon in the filling. Roll it up, folding in the bottom like a cigar with one end pinched shut, to catch the juices. Repeat with remaining tortillas. Serve at once.

great salsa verde calzone

Now that you can buy pizza dough in the refrigerated section, the possibilities expand for quick dinners that are bound to please children of all ages. Besides the usual pizza, which is as quick as a can of biscuits, try folding the dough around a savory filling for a jiffy calzone. Too good.

8 anchovy fillets, drained

2 garlic cloves, chopped

¾ cup packed fresh flat-leaf parsley leaves

½ cup celery

2 tablespoons extra-virgin olive oil

1 tablespoon balsamic vinegar

1 pound fully cooked beef crumbles

Salt and freshly milled pepper

1 ball refrigerated pizza dough

1 cup shredded mozzarella cheese

makes 3 to 5 servings
time: 25 minutes

1 Preheat the oven to 400° F.

2 Make the filling.
In a food processor, combine the anchovies, garlic, parsley, and celery, and pulse to chop coarsely. Add the oil and vinegar, and process for about 30 seconds, until well blended. Add the beef crumbles and salt and pepper to taste.

3 Fill and bake the calzone.
Spritz a baking sheet with vegetable oil cooking spray. Roll out the pizza dough directly on the baking sheet into a large circle. Spoon all the filling onto one side, top with the cheese, and then fold in half to make a large semicircle. Seal, crimping the edges to prevent leakage. Bake until golden brown, about 20 minutes. Let it stand a few moments; then cut into wedges to serve.

ground lamb and tomato
cinnamon sauce and corn

Ground lamb is a refreshing change from ground beef. Cinnamon is used with lamb in many Middle Eastern dishes and works well with its strong flavor all sitting neatly on a bed of sweet (formerly frozen) corn. In a pinch, substitute cooked ground beef.

1 (16-ounce) bag frozen corn

2 tablespoons water

2 tablespoons (¼ stick) butter

2 tablespoons olive oil

1 pound ground lamb (or buy ground beef crumbles)

1 cup chopped onion

2 cloves garlic, finely chopped

1 teaspoon ground cinnamon

1 (28-ounce) can tomatoes, chopped, with their juice

Salt and freshly milled pepper

makes 4 servings
time: 20 minutes

1 Warm up the corn.

Place the corn, water, and butter in a large bowl, and microwave on HIGH (100 percent power) for 7 minutes.

2 Meanwhile make the lamb sauce.

Coat a large heavy skillet with the olive oil, and heat over medium-high heat for 1 minute. Stir in the lamb, onion, garlic, and cinnamon, and brown for 10 minutes, or until the lamb is thoroughly cooked.

3 Deglaze the pan.

Stir the tomatoes and their juice into the browned lamb, scraping up the browned bits from the bottom of the pan. Season to taste with salt and pepper.

4 Arrange the dish.

Drain the corn, and spread it out on a large platter. Spoon the lamb mixture over the corn, and serve.

middle eastern salad with
lamb and pita triangles

Pitas freeze so well. We keep them on hand for those now-expected culinary crises.

Dressing

- 1 garlic clove, chopped
- ¼ cup fresh lemon juice
- ¼ cup extra-virgin olive oil
- Salt and freshly milled pepper

makes 4 servings
time: 25 minutes

Lamb

- 1½ pounds ground lamb
- 2 cloves garlic, chopped
- Salt and freshly milled pepper
- 2 tablespoons olive oil

Salad

- 1 head romaine lettuce, chopped coarsely
- ½ cup chopped scallions
- ½ cup chopped fresh mint leaves, stems discarded
- ½ cup chopped fresh flat-leaf parsley
- 3 (8-inch pitas), cut into 6 triangles, toasted

1 Mix the salad dressing.

Stir together the garlic, lemon juice, olive oil, and salt and pepper to taste.

2 Cook the meat.

In a bowl, toss the lamb, garlic, and salt and pepper to taste with 1 tablespoon of the oil. Place a dry medium black skillet over medium-high heat for 2 minutes. Add the remaining 1 tablespoon of olive oil, and heat for 1 more minute. Toss in the meat, and cook it for 6 to 10 minutes, until thoroughly browned.

3 Arrange the salad.

Toss the lettuce, scallions, mint, parsley, and toasted pita triangles with the dressing (holding some dressing for the cooked lamb) on a large platter or bowl. Top with the lamb, and drizzle the lamb with the remaining dressing.

thirty-minute turkey mole stew

In the Southwest, this is considered "strong food," guaranteed to make you feel better. Using canned beans and chili powder, it makes you better fast. Thanks to the influx of Mexican immigrants, you'll find jars of mole in the Mexican section of grocery stores coast to coast.

1 tablespoon olive oil	
1½ pounds ground turkey	
1 cup frozen chopped onion	
4 garlic cloves, smashed	
1 large green bell pepper, chopped	
1 (4.25-ounce) jar chopped green chiles	
2 tablespoons chili powder (Gebhardt's is best)	
1 (6-ounce) jar mole sauce	
1 (1-ounce) square unsweetened baking chocolate	
2 (14½-ounce) cans low-sodium fat-free chicken broth	
1 (14½-ounce) can chopped tomatoes	
1 (19-ounce) can black turtle beans	
½ cup raisins	
½ teaspoon salt	
½ teaspoon pepper	
Tortilla chips	
½ cup chopped cilantro	

makes 8 servings
time: 30 minutes or less

1 Cook the meat with spices.

In a large soup pot, heat the oil over medium heat, and brown the turkey, adding the onion, garlic, bell pepper, chiles, and chili powder as you prepare it, about 10 minutes total, stirring. Add the mole, chocolate, broth, tomatoes, beans, and raisins. Simmer for about 20 minutes, stirring to make sure the chocolate and mole have thoroughly dissolved. Season to taste with salt and pepper.

2 Serve the stew.

Serve the turkey mole stew in bowls, sprinkled with tortilla chips and chopped cilantro.

fully cooked roasts and meatballs

The traditional all-American dinner main courses, including roast beef and meatballs, are ready to go in the fresh meat counter and sometimes in the frozen food department. Here again, due to the nature of the meat business, where most meat processors are local, you will have to try out different brands to find the best one available in your area. Don't be fooled by fancy packaging. Our favorite Italian meatballs are made by a local concern and packaged very simply. A big national brand we tried would be best used to throw at magicians who aren't doing their job. Be picky. It's your family we're talking about here. Gotta feed 'em right.

1. **Italian Meatball Stew with Orange and Basil**

2. **Meatballs with Spiced Brandy Cream Sauce**

3. **Belgian Beef Stew**

4. **Beef Bourguignonne**

5. **Beef Curry**

6. **Beef Paprikash**

7. **Baked Balsamic Beef with Winter Vegetables**

8. **Barbecued Pork Buns with Coleslaw**

italian meatball stew with orange and basil

Keep a package of frozen Italian meatballs on hand for a quick, rich vegetable stew. It's guaranteed to soothe your soul when the wind blows and the mercury drops. Add a crusty loaf, pop open a bottle of Chianti, and you're ready for a long winter's night.

1 tablespoon extra-virgin olive oil

1 cup chopped onion

2 tablespoons all-purpose flour

1 cup dry vermouth

1 (16-ounce) can chicken broth

1 (14½-ounce) can chopped tomatoes and juice

1 (12-ounce) package frozen Italian meatballs

¼ cup chopped fresh basil (1 tablespoon dried)

½ teaspoon thyme

Juice and julienned zest of 1 orange

3 cloves garlic, smashed

½ pound cremini or button mushrooms, trimmed and quartered

Kosher salt and pepper

Fresh basil leaves or flat-leaf parsley (for garnish)

makes 8 servings
time: 20 minutes

1 Sauté the vegetables.
In a stew pot, heat the oil over medium heat; then add the onion, and sauté until golden, about 3 minutes. Sprinkle with flour, and continue cooking and stirring until the flour begins to brown, about 2 minutes.

2 Make the stew.
Deglaze the pan with the vermouth (scraping up browned bits); then add the broth, tomatoes and juice, meatballs, basil, thyme, orange juice and zest, garlic, and mushrooms. Raise to a boil; then reduce the heat and simmer, uncovered, until the mushrooms are cooked through, about 10 minutes. Season to taste with salt and pepper.

3 Serve.
Ladle the stew into soup bowls garnished with basil or parsley.

meatballs with spiced brandy cream sauce

This recipe might almost qualify as embarrassing because it's so easy to throw together. Whipping cream is surprisingly stable. All that fat gives it great shelf life, and we find that it will last up to three weeks if unopened. It always adds a silky texture and is a great flavor conductor.

3	tablespoons butter
1	onion, chopped
2	tablespoons all-purpose flour
2	cups wild mushrooms, fresh or frozen
1	(10½-ounce) can beef broth
½	cup white wine
½	teaspoon ground allspice
16 to 20	frozen beef meatballs (either Swedish or Italian)
½	cup whipping cream
2	tablespoons brandy
	Salt and freshly milled pepper
	Cooked egg noodles, rice, or couscous

makes 4 servings
time: 20 minutes

1 Make the sauce.

In a heavy soup pan or Dutch oven, melt the butter over medium heat. Stir in the onion, and cook for 3 minutes over medium-low heat. Whisk in the flour, and stir for 1 to 2 minutes, until the flour begins to turn golden brown. Stir in the mushrooms, broth, wine, and allspice, and bring to a boil.

2 Finish the dish.

Add the meatballs, cover, and simmer on medium heat for 15 minutes. Stir in the whipping cream and brandy, and cook for 10 more minutes. Taste and adjust the seasoning with the salt and pepper. Serve with egg noodles, rice, or couscous.

belgian beef stew

Beer is a wonderful flavor enhancer and a key ingredient in the traditional carbonnade, a quick and easy version of which we pull together in minutes using pre-cooked pot roast. The beer adds a rich and yeasty flavor you'll find most appealing even if you're not a suds-lover. Serve this with noodles.

2 tablespoons extra-virgin olive oil

1 large onion, chopped

2 stalks celery, chopped

1 cup chopped carrots

4 garlic cloves, chopped

2 tablespoons all-purpose flour

1 bottle dark beer

1 pound ready-cooked pot roast, gravy reserved, pulled into bite-size chunks

2 tablespoons chopped fresh rosemary

makes 6 servings
time: 25 minutes

1 Sauté the vegetables.

Coat the bottom of a large Dutch oven with the olive oil. Over medium-high heat, cook the onion, celery, and carrots until the vegetables are softened, about 4 minutes. Add the garlic, and sauté for 1 more minute. Stir in the flour, and cook for another 2 to 3 minutes, or until the flour begins to turn golden brown.

2 Deglaze the pan.

Stir in the beer, scraping up the browned bits from the bottom of the pan. Bring to a boil, and add the beef and its gravy; stir thoroughly.

3 Finish the stew.

Stir in the rosemary, reduce the heat to low, and simmer for 15 minutes.

beef bourguignonne

Who knew this classic could be made in under an hour—or half an hour, for that matter? Made with frozen mushrooms and baby carrots (no peeling!), the dish involves virtually no prep work. Magnifique!

2 tablespoons extra-virgin olive oil

3 slices bacon, chopped

1½ cups frozen pearl onions, thawed

2 cups wild mushrooms, fresh or frozen, thawed

1 cup baby carrots

4 garlic cloves, chopped

2 tablespoons all-purpose flour

1 (750 ml) bottle dry red wine

1 pound ready-cooked pot roast, gravy reserved, pulled into bite-size chunks

½ cup chopped fresh thyme leaves

makes 6 servings
time: 25 minutes

1 Sauté the bacon and vegetables.

Coat the bottom of a large Dutch oven with the olive oil. Cook the chopped bacon over medium-high heat for about 2 minutes, until it is translucent but not crisp. Add the onions, mushrooms, carrots, and garlic, and sauté, stirring fairly often. Stir in the flour, and cook for another 2 to 3 minutes, until the flour begins to turn golden brown.

2 Deglaze the pan.

Stir in the wine, scraping up the browned bits from the bottom of the pan. Bring to a boil, and add the cubed beef and its gravy. Stir thoroughly.

3 Finish the stew.

Stir in the thyme, reduce the heat to low, and simmer for 20 minutes.

beef curry

Curry powder, ready-mixed to perfection, improves almost anything it is added to. Using a ready-cooked pot roast, you can have beef curry in minutes with plenty of deep, rich flavor.

makes 6 servings
time: 25 minutes

2 tablespoons vegetable oil

1 large onion, chopped

1 tablespoon curry powder

2 large tomatoes, chopped

2 garlic cloves, chopped

2 tablespoons minced fresh ginger

Hot red pepper flakes

1 cup beef or chicken broth

1 pound ready-cooked pot roast, gravy reserved, pulled into bite-size chunks

4 cups cooked basmati or white rice

1 Sauté the soup base.

Coat the bottom of a large Dutch oven with the oil. Cook the onion over medium-high heat for 2 to 3 minutes, until it begins to turn translucent. Add the curry powder, tomatoes, garlic, ginger, and a few red pepper flakes to taste, and continue to cook until blended, about 4 minutes.

2 Deglaze the pan.

Stir in the broth, scraping up the browned bits from the bottom of the pan. Bring to a boil, and add the beef and its gravy; stir thoroughly.

3 Finish the stew.

Reduce the heat to low, and simmer for 15 minutes. Taste, and adjust the seasonings. Serve over rice.

beef paprikash

Paprika is an underappreciated spice in this country, where many consider it nothing more than a garnish for deviled eggs. The good stuff, both Hungarian sweet or Spanish spicy, can really add sweet or smoky flavor.

2 tablespoons extra-virgin olive oil

1 large onion, chopped

1 large green bell pepper, chopped

2 cups frozen wild mushrooms, thawed

1 tablespoon tomato paste

2 tablespoons all-purpose flour

1 tablespoon Hungarian sweet paprika (or Spanish paprika)

2 (16-ounce) cans beef broth

1 pound ready-cooked pot roast, gravy reserved, pulled into bite-size chunks

12 ounces egg noodles

2 tablespoons unsalted butter

1 cup sour cream

makes 4 servings
time: 20 minutes

1 Sauté the vegetables.

Coat the bottom of a large Dutch oven with the olive oil. Cook the onion, green pepper, mushrooms, and tomato paste for about 4 minutes over medium-high heat, until the vegetables are softened. Stir in the flour and paprika, and cook for another 2 to 3 minutes, until the flour begins to turn golden brown.

2 Deglaze the pan.

Stir in the beef broth, scraping up the browned bits from the bottom of the pan. Bring to a boil, and add the cubed beef and its gravy; stir thoroughly. Reduce the heat to low, and simmer for 10 minutes.

3 Make the noodles.

In a large pot, bring 3 quarts of water to a boil. Cook the noodles until tender; then drain and return to the pot. Add the butter, and toss until melted.

4 Finish the stew.

Stir in the sour cream, and remove the pan from the heat. Serve the stew over the buttered egg noodles.

baked balsamic beef with
winter vegetables

Talk about no trouble. Throw this in the oven for a few minutes to allow the flavors to marry, and it's done. Use the microwave for one of its favorite tasks: quick-cooking vegetables. Stir the veggies into the stew, and it's time to eat.

4 bacon slices

1 teaspoon maple syrup

1/2 pound cremini mushrooms, trimmed and quartered

6 garlic cloves

2 cups frozen pearl onions

1 pound baby carrots

1 fully cooked pot roast (2 to 3 pounds), pulled into bite-size chunks

3 tablespoons balsamic vinegar

1 (10 1/2-ounce) can French onion soup

1 tablespoon tomato paste

2 bay leaves

1 tablespoon thyme

1 tablespoon sage

1 tablespoon rosemary

1/2 teaspoon kosher salt

1/2 teaspoon freshly milled pepper

1/4 cup fine, dry bread crumbs

1/2 cup chopped fresh parsley (for garnish)

makes 8 servings
time: 30 minutes

1 Prepare the bacon and vegetables.

Preheat the oven to 350°F. Arrange the bacon on a rack over a baking sheet, and cook until crisp, about 5 minutes. Turn the bacon slices once, and brush them with maple syrup. Cook for 5 minutes longer. Remove the bacon from the oven. Crumble the bacon, and reserve. Toss mushrooms, garlic cloves, pearl onions, and carrots in the bacon drippings until cooled.

2 Bake the roast.

Raise the oven temperature to 500°F. In a 3-quart covered casserole, combine the beef chunks with the vinegar and soup. Stir in the tomato paste and 2 cups of water; then add the bay leaves, thyme, sage, and rosemary. Season to taste with the salt and pepper. Sprinkle with bread crumbs. Cover, and bake for 15 minutes, or until the sauce has thickened.

3 Cook the vegetables.

At the same time, cook the vegetable mixture uncovered in the microwave with ½ cup of water until the carrots are tender, about 5 minutes. Drain and stir into the beef, along with the crumbled bacon. Return the casserole to the oven, and bake for 15 minutes more to blend the flavors.

4 Serve.

Garnish with the parsley and serve in rimmed soup bowls accompanied by crusty bread.

barbecued pork buns with coleslaw

Authentic South Carolina–style pulled pork sandwiches start with six hours of slow-smoking and long-cooking of barbecue sauce. Groan. Fortunately, it's a snap to create them from barbecued pork that comes in a tub. All you need to add are bakery corn muffins or muffins made from those little boxes of corn-bread mix and a pint of deli coleslaw. If you don't use all the pork at once, freeze the remainder in the tub for up to 3 months.

1 (16-ounce) tub chopped pork barbecue in sauce

8 small warm corn muffins

1 pint deli coleslaw

makes 4 servings
time: 10 minutes

1 Heat the pork.

Following package directions, heat the barbecue in the microwave or stovetop just to a simmer. Remove from the heat.

2 Make the sandwiches.

Cut muffins in half, and arrange them on 4 plates. Add a generous serving of pork barbecue to each one. Top with a spoonful of coleslaw, and add the muffin tops. Serve immediately.

chapter two *
from the dairy case

Think dinner from the dairy case means eating yogurt out of the container? Think again. There are half-scratch miracles sprinkled up and down that chilly aisle, from prerolled (or preformed) pastry dough to our current obsession, tubes of ready-to-serve polenta. Each of these makes a tasty and truly home-cooked base for lots of savory toppings. We bet you'll find the recipes that follow are just the thing to get you thinking up your own toppers and combos. And while you're at it, take that pizza delivery number off your speed dial.

prepared crusts: your secret

A sandwich is fine for a quick bite, but put something good in or on a crust—be it of the pastry, pita, pizza, or phyllo variety—and suddenly you're talking a meal. A pre-rolled, neatly folded refrigerator crust stashed in your fridge can be the beginning of a world of suppers. In our opinion, these are far superior to any frozen product that's already formed, and they preserve the illusion of homemade far better, too. And if you don't know about mini phyllo dough shells yet, you're in for a treat. These tiny wonders don't even require refrigeration, so you can have them waiting for the next time guests appear at your door without warning. Just pop open a package, fill them with whatever you have on hand, and it's a party.

You probably have already discovered prebaked pizza crusts, and you'll find some new ways to jazz them up here, but we're also fans of rising crust pizzas that you'll find in the freezer case. Often thought of as the food of bachelors, frozen pizzas make a terrific base for food on bread. Tortillas and wraps made into interesting quesadillas in the microwave are on the table in two minutes. Middle Easterners have been using pitas for their version of pizza for centuries. Here are a few of our favorites. You may wonder why we specify Boboli. It is a product with no peer. We tried 'em all, and that's our fave. You like another? Go for it.

1. Hollandaise Asparagus Tart

2. Pacific Rim Quiche

3. Wild Mushroom Quiche

4. Six Tricks to Perform with a
      Prepared Piecrust

5. Mini Phyllo Dough Shells Filled with
      Tomato and Olives

6. Bruschetta Pizza with Sun-Dried
      Tomato and Sausage

7. Antipasto Pizza

8. Balsamic-Glazed Chicken Pizza
      with Roasted Garlic

9. Pizza with Barbecued Chicken and
      Cheddar Cheese

10. Pizza with Mozzarella and Fresh Arugula

11. Pizza with Lime Chicken and Salsa

12. Smoked Turkey, Artichoke Heart,
      and Pesto Pizza

13. Caribbean Shrimp Pita-Pizza

hollandaise-asparagus tart

Sinfully rich and eggy, with a lemony tang, this glorious yellow-and-green savory tart is easy and full flavored. Flecked with tarragon and accented by a wheel of roasted asparagus, the golden tart is a winner.

1 refrigerator piecrust

1 teaspoon all-purpose flour

1 pound fresh asparagus, cut into 3½-inch lengths (discard stems)

⅔ cup half-and-half

2 large eggs

2 tablespoons fresh lemon juice

Grated zest of ½ lemon

½ cup grated Parmesan cheese

1 teaspoon dried tarragon (1 tablespoon fresh)

½ teaspoon salt

makes 4 to 6 servings
time: 55 minutes or less

1 Preheat the oven to 450° F.

2 Prepare the piecrust.
Open the crust onto a work surface, and rub with the flour, pressing out any cracks. Transfer the crust to a 9-inch tart pan with a removable bottom. Press the dough into the pan, folding the excess under to form a double-thick side-wall. Pierce the dough all over with a fork. Bake until it is golden, 10 to 15 minutes. Cool the crust in the pan on a rack.

3 Prepare the asparagus.
Meanwhile, steam the asparagus tips over boiling water just until crisp-tender, about 3 minutes. Lift the steamer out of the pan, and run cold water over the asparagus to set the color. Cool on paper towels.

4 Make the filling.
Whisk together the half-and-half, eggs, lemon juice, lemon zest, cheese, tarragon, and salt. Arrange the asparagus in the crust, and add the filling.

5 Serve.
Bake until the tart puffs and the top browns, about 30 minutes. Cool for 10 minutes; then cut into 6 wedges and serve warm or at room temperature.

pacific rim quiche

Seafood pie is the epitome of elegant brunch fare and a very refined supper dish. Start with a frozen bag of shrimp with stir-fry vegetables. (We love Trader Joe's house brand.) You'll have this brightly colored quiche on the table impressing your guests before they can name the principal countries of the Pacific Rim.

1 (16-ounce) package frozen shrimp or seafood stir-fry

1 refrigerator piecrust

1 teaspoon all-purpose flour

6 large eggs

makes 4 servings
time: 37 minutes

1 Preheat the oven to 425°F.

2 Cook the frozen shrimp or seafood stir-fry.

Place the frozen stir-fry in a large glass or ceramic bowl in the microwave on HIGH (100 percent power) for 5 minutes.

3 Prepare the piecrust.

Open the crust onto a work surface, and rub it with flour, pressing out any cracks. Transfer the crust to a 9-inch tart pan with a removable bottom. Press the dough into the pan, folding the excess under to form a double-thick sidewall. Pierce the dough all over with a fork. Bake until it is golden, 10 to 15 minutes. Cool the crust in the pan on a rack.

4 Finish the filling.

Pour the cooked stir-fry into the crust. Beat in the eggs, and pour the filling into the pie.

5 Cook the quiche.

Place the quiche on the center rack of the oven, and cook for 20 minutes. Cool for 10 minutes on a rack, then cut into wedges.

wild mushroom quiche

Using the ready-made fondue mixture greatly improves the texture of this brunch standby. The complex flavor of the wild mushrooms complemented by the wine and Swiss cheese is fabulous.

1 refrigerator piecrust

1 teaspoon all-purpose flour

7 ounces (½ package) frozen cheese fondue

½ pound frozen wild mushrooms (or marinated mushrooms)

½ teaspoon thyme

½ cup milk

5 large eggs

makes 4 servings
time: 40 minutes

1 Preheat the oven to 425° F.

2 Prepare the piecrust.
Open the crust onto a work surface, and rub it with flour, pressing out any cracks. Transfer the crust to a 9-inch tart pan with a removable bottom. Press the dough into the pan, folding the excess under to form a double-thick side-wall. Pierce the dough all over with a fork. Bake until it is golden, 10 to 15 minutes. Cool the crust in the pan on a rack.

3 Make the filling.
Place the cheese mixture and mushrooms in a large glass or ceramic bowl in the microwave on HIGH (100 percent power) for 2 minutes. Stir in the thyme and milk, and continue to cook in the microwave on HIGH for 5 minutes. Pour the mixture into the pie crust.

4 Finish the quiche.
Beat the eggs, and stir them into the pie. Place the quiche on the center rack of the oven, and bake it for 20 minutes. Cool the quiche on a wire rack for 10 minutes or so.

5 Serve.
Cut into 4 wedges, and serve warm.

Six Tricks to Perform with a Prepared Piecrust

Start by heating the oven to 400°F; then, using a frozen crust in a pie tin (thawed) or 1 refrigerator piecrust (crimp the edges) and your own pie pan, bake the empty crust for 5 minutes. Reduce the temperature to 375°F, and add one of the fillings below. Bake for 30 minutes.

1.**Quiche Lorraine.** Crumble cooked bacon (try the precooked strips of real bacon) with 1 cup chopped frozen onion, and place the mixture in the prebaked pie crust. Whisk 2 eggs together with ⅔ cup half-and-half, and pour it into the crust. Season with salt and pepper. Top with 1 cup shredded Swiss cheese, and bake.

2.**Quiche du Jour.** Wilt 3 cups of triple-washed spinach in a skillet with cooked, chopped bacon and onion over medium heat. Place in the prebaked piecrust. Add 2 eggs as directed in Recipe 1. Top with 1 cup shredded mozzarella cheese, and bake. Substitute vegetables at will.

3.**Vegetable Pie.** Toss together ½ cup shredded Cheddar and ½ cup shredded Swiss cheese with ½ cup shredded carrot, 2 sliced scallions, and 1 clove garlic, pressed. Place the filling in the prebaked piecrust. Add 2 eggs as directed in Recipe 1. Season with salt and pepper. Top with ⅔ cup sour cream, and bake.

4.**Crab Soufflé.** Combine 6½ ounces cooked fresh crabmeat with ½ cup sliced scallions, 1 tablespoon dry sherry, and 1 cup shredded Swiss cheese. Place the filling in the prebaked piecrust. Add 2 eggs as directed in Recipe 1. Sprinkle top with ½ cup seasoned bread crumbs. Bake.

5.**Chile Rellenos Pie.** Combine 1 cup shredded Jack cheese with 1 (4½-ounce) can chopped green chiles, 1 chopped green or red bell pepper, and 1 minced fresh jalapeño pepper. Pour the mixture into the prepared piecrust. Add 2 eggs as directed in Recipe 1. Season with salt and pepper. Top with ½ cup shredded Cheddar cheese. Bake. Serve with a side of sour cream and fresh salsa.

6.**Ham and Cheese Pie.** Stir together 1 cup chopped cooked ham with 5 ounces (half a 10-ounce package) frozen broccoli, ¼ cup frozen chopped onions, and 1 tablespoon Dijon mustard. Pour the mixture into the prebaked piecrust. Add 2 eggs as directed in Recipe 1. Top with 1 cup shredded sharp Cheddar cheese. Bake.

mini phyllo dough shells filled with tomato and olives

For nearly instant hors d'oeuvres, fill those cute little shells with ready-to-go bruschetta mix topped with a black olive. They make a yummy mouthful. If your grocer doesn't stock these yet, ask him to get them for you. We buy the ones from Fillo Factory and love 'em.

1 (15-shell) package mini phyllo shells

1 cup ready-made bruschetta topping*

15 black olives, halved lengthwise

makes 4 to 5 servings
time: 15 minutes

1 Preheat the oven to 350° F.

2 Bake the shells.
Place the shells on a cookie sheet, and place it on the center rack of the oven. Bake for 3 to 5 minutes, until the edges begin to brown.

3 Fill the shells.
Fill each shell with 2 teaspoons of the bruschetta mix and 2 black olive halves.

* You can make your own bruschetta topping by folding together 2 cups chopped ripe tomatoes with ¼ cup olive oil, 1 chopped garlic clove, and 6 basil leaves torn into small pieces.

bruschetta pizza with sun-dried tomato and sausage

Fresh tasting with big chunks of tomato, heavy with sausage, and extra cheesy, this puts the old pepperoni standard to shame.

1 frozen rising-crust cheese pizza

¾ pound fully cooked chicken sausage (we like one with sun-dried tomatoes and basil)

2 cups ready-made bruschetta topping*

½ cup pitted kalamata olives, sliced

¼ cup freshly grated Parmesan cheese

makes 4 servings
time: 25 minutes

1 Bake the pizza.

Preheat the oven, and bake the pizza according to the package instructions, minus 10 minutes.

2 Cook the sausage.

While the pizza is baking, cook the sausage in the microwave oven on HIGH (100 percent power) for 1 to 2 minutes, until heated through. Slice into ¼-inch rounds. Lay the slices on a layer of paper towels to drain.

3 Top the pizza.

Remove the pizza from the oven 10 minutes before the baking is through. Spread it with the bruschetta mixture; then top with the sausage and olives. Sprinkle with the Parmesan. Return the pizza to the oven for the final 10 minutes of baking. Serve hot.

* You can make your own bruschetta topping by folding together 2 cups chopped ripe tomatoes with ¼ cup olive oil, 1 chopped garlic clove, and 6 basil leaves torn into small pieces.

antipasto pizza

Here is a great way to improve a frozen pizza—plus you get the salad and dinner on one dish. Can't find basil oil? You know what to do: Crush basil leaves in extra-virgin olive oil.

1 large frozen rising-crust cheese pizza, preferably 4-cheese variety

3 cups mesclun greens, washed and dried

¾ cup (4 ounces) roasted red peppers from a jar, drained and cut into ¼-inch-wide strips

¼ cup marinated mushrooms, sliced thin

1 small ripe tomato, cored and diced

1 tablespoon white balsamic vinegar

1 tablespoon olive oil, preferably basil-infused

makes 4 servings
time: 25 minutes

1 Bake the pizza.

Preheat the oven, and bake the pizza according to the package instructions.

2 Top the pizza.

Remove the pizza from the oven, and top with the mesclun greens, red peppers, mushrooms, and tomato. Drizzle balsamic vinegar and olive oil over the top. Serve immediately.

balsamic-glazed chicken pizza with roasted garlic

Reminiscent of a certain prize-winning, best-selling chain pizza, this is easy to assemble at home.

2 large frozen rising-crust cheese pizzas

1 (11-ounce) package sliced honey-roasted chicken breast

½ cup roasted garlic and balsamic marinade

½ cup roasted garlic purée (available at gourmet markets in a tube or jar)

makes 4 servings
time: 25 minutes

1 Bake the pizzas.
Preheat the oven, and bake the pizzas according to the package instructions, minus 10 minutes.

2 Make the topping.
While the pizzas are baking, prepare the topping. In a medium bowl, stir together the chicken, roasted garlic and balsamic marinade, and the garlic purée. Mix well to coat the chicken evenly.

3 Top the pizzas.
Remove the pizzas from the oven 10 minutes before the baking is through. Mound half the chicken mixture on each pizza. Return the pizzas to the oven for the final 10 minutes of baking. Cut each pizza in quarters, and serve 2 pieces per person.

pizza with barbecued chicken and cheddar cheese

This is an interesting twist on a pizza. A version joining ubiquitous barbecue sauce and chicken made the California Pizza Kitchen's reputation. Mild Cheddar cheese nicely compliments the flavor with crunchy scallions as an interesting textural twist, and you can make it at home in less time than it takes to order in.

2 (12-ounce) packages roasted sliced chicken breasts

1 cup barbecue sauce

1 (12-inch) prebaked thin pizza crust, such as Boboli

2 cups grated Cheddar cheese

2 scallions, chopped

makes 4 servings
time: 25 minutes

1 Preheat the oven to 450° F.

2 Top the pizza.
In a medium bowl, mix the chicken pieces and barbecue sauce together. Arrange the chicken on the pizza crust, and top with the Cheddar cheese. Place the pizza directly on the center oven rack with a cookie sheet on the rack below to catch any spills.

3 Cook the pizza.
Bake for 10 to 15 minutes. Top with the chopped scallions, and serve hot.

pizza with mozzarella and fresh arugula

This idea comes from a pizzeria in Carroll Gardens, one of the last Italian strong-holds in Brooklyn. The contrast of warm pizza and cold arugula is stunning. Try it with fresh mozzarella for an extra treat. The convenience of having your salad on top of the pizza isn't bad either.

1 (12-inch) prebaked thin pizza crust (such as Boboli)

1 cup marinara sauce

½ cup pitted kalamata olives, sliced

2 cups grated mozzarella cheese

1 (10-ounce) package or bunch arugula

makes 4 servings
time: 25 minutes

1 Preheat the oven to 450° F.

2 Top the pizza.
Layer the pizza crust with the sauce, olives, and cheese.

3 Cook the pizza.
Place the pizza directly on the center oven rack with a cookie sheet on the rack below to catch any spills. Bake for 10 to 15 minutes.

4 Serve.
Top with the fresh arugula, and serve immediately.

pizza with lime chicken and salsa

Did you know that salsa has replaced ketchup as the condiment most commonly found in America's refrigerators? It's true, and it's great on pizza, too. Top with avocado slices. It will knock your socks off.

2 (12-ounce) packages cooked chicken cuts

   Juice and zest of 1 lime

1 (12-inch) prepared thin crust pizza crust (such as Boboli)

2 cups mild fresh or prepared salsa

2 cups grated Monterey Jack cheese

2 scallions, chopped, both white and green parts

1 avocado, pitted and sliced

makes 4 servings
time: 25 minutes

1 Preheat the oven to 450° F.

2 Top the pizza.

In a medium bowl, mix together the chicken pieces and the lime juice and zest. Layer the pizza crust with the salsa, the seasoned chicken, and then the Jack cheese.

3 Cook the pizza.

Place the pizza directly on the center oven rack with a cookie sheet on the rack below to catch any spills. Bake for 10 to 15 minutes. Top with the scallions and avocado. Serve hot.

smoked turkey, artichoke heart, and pesto pizza

Dash into the grocery store for pesto, deli smoked turkey, artichoke hearts, some mozzarella, and a Boboli crust, and you have an interesting dinner fixable in twenty-five minutes.

1 (12-inch) prebaked thin pizza crust (such as Boboli)

1 tablespoon olive oil

$\frac{1}{2}$ cup prepared pesto*

2 cups ($\frac{1}{4}$ pound) smoked turkey cut into $\frac{1}{4}$-inch strips

1 ($6\frac{1}{2}$-ounce) jar marinated artichoke hearts, drained and sliced

2 cups grated mozzarella cheese

makes 4 servings
time: 25 minutes

1 Preheat the oven to 450° F.

2 Top the pizza.
Brush the top of the crust with the olive oil, and spread it with the pesto. Layer the turkey strips, sliced artichokes, and grated mozzarella onto the crust.

3 Cook the pizza.
Place the crust directly on the center oven rack with a baking sheet on the rack below to catch any drips. Bake for 10 to 15 minutes. Serve hot.

---

* Want to make your own? Pack a food processor with about 2 cups basil leaves, $\frac{1}{4}$ cup pine nuts, 2 cloves garlic, a pinch of salt, and $\frac{1}{4}$ cup Parmesan cheese. Process, drizzling in $\frac{1}{2}$ cup extra-virgin olive oil, until you have a rough purée. Store in the refrigerator or freezer, covered. Keeps for 1 week in the cool part, 3 months frozen.

caribbean shrimp pita-pizza

Don't even have time to preheat the oven? Simply assemble this colorful no-cook pizza, and dig in. Sweet little bay shrimp defrost in minutes, or buy them ready to use at the deli.

1 pound cleaned, cooked bay shrimp

$\frac{2}{3}$ cup Lime Mango Chutney Mayonnaise (page 183)

2 pocketless pita breads

2 cups shredded romaine lettuce

2 scallions, sliced

makes 4 servings
time: 10 minutes

1 Dress the shrimp.

In a small bowl, toss the shrimp with the Lime-Mango Chutney Mayonnaise. Keep refrigerated until ready to use.

2 Assemble the pita.

On each pita spread 1 cup of the shredded lettuce and half the shrimp salad mixture. Top with the scallions, and serve.

polenta in a tube

We love polenta in a tube. This ready-to-go starch base, found in the refrigerated case of most markets, delivers good flavor, vivid color, and great texture. It makes an outstanding base for individual-serving casseroles, and the earthy corn flavor marries well with a variety of ingredients while holding its own.

Mini-casseroles have several distinct advantages: being small means that they heat up more quickly in the oven, cutting down on the cooking time. And they make an elegant, restaurant-style presentation. Allow two servings for a main course, one as a first course or if you are serving a bunch of side dishes. Here are eight different variations, but we invite you to try your own, as well. Choose individual ramekins, Pyrex custard cups, or other mini-dishes as vessels to hold your individual casseroles. We sometimes mix and match patterns and sizes so the table will look interesting. Short on ramekins? Make side-by-side stacks in a baking dish just large enough to hold them.

1. Chicken Enchiladas in a Cup

2. Salsa-Guacamole Napoleons

3. Caponata and Smoked Gouda Mini-Casseroles

4. Black Bean and Goat Cheese Polenta Casseroles

5. Individual Polenta Lasagnas

6. Barbecued Pork and Mango Chutney Mini-Casseroles

7. Pesto Chicken and Polenta Mini-Casseroles

8. Ginger Chicken and Polenta Mini-Casseroles

chicken enchiladas in a cup

Serve these delightful Mexican-influenced casseroles with a side of chopped iceberg lettuce dressed with a lemony vinaigrette and a couple of microwaved flour tortillas and butter along with a well-chilled cerveza.

1 (16-ounce) tube ready-cooked polenta, sliced into 16 (½-inch-thick) medallions

1 (10-ounce) package (2 cups) cooked chicken (we like cooked carved chicken breast)

4 scallions, chopped

1 (10-ounce) can mild enchilada sauce

1 cup grated sharp Cheddar cheese

½ cup sour cream (for garnish)

makes 4 servings
time: 25 minutes

1 **Preheat the oven to 425° F.**

2 **Make the casseroles.**
Spray 8 (12-ounce) ramekins with cooking spray. In each one, layer 1 polenta medallion, 2 tablespoons of the chicken, 1 tablespoon of the scallions, 1 tablespoon of the enchilada sauce, 2 tablespoons of the grated cheese, a second polenta medallion, another shot of the enchilada sauce, and more cheese.

3 **Bake the ramekins.**
Set the ramekins on a cookie sheet to prevent spills. Place the ramekins on the center rack of the oven, and bake for 15 minutes, until hot and bubbly.

4 **Garnish the casseroles.**
Garnish each ramekin with 1 tablespoon of the sour cream, and sprinkle with the remaining scallions. Serve hot, 2 ramekins per person.

salsa-guacamole napoleons

Fresh salsa and cilantro give these quick hunger quenchers a fresh perspective. The mild flavor of Monterey Jack and the suave, nutty flavor of polenta are complemented by the spicy salsa. Serve with a dollop of ready-to-go guacamole.

1 (16-ounce) tube ready-cooked polenta, sliced into 16 (½-inch-thick) medallions

1 (10-ounce) package (2 cups) chopped cooked chicken (rotisserie bird or cooked carved chicken breast)

2 cups mild fresh or prepared salsa

1 cup grated Monterey Jack cheese

1 bunch cilantro leaves, coarsely chopped (for garnish)

½ cup prepared guacamole or 1 avocado, sliced

makes 4 servings
time: 25 minutes

1 Preheat the oven to 425°F.

2 Make the casseroles.

Spray 8 (12-ounce) ramekins with cooking spray, and in each one, layer 1 polenta medallion, ¼ cup of the chicken, 2 tablespoons of the salsa, 2 tablespoons of the Monterey Jack cheese, a second polenta medallion, and 1 more tablespoon of salsa, plus more cheese.

3 Bake the ramekins.

Set the ramekins on a cookie sheet to prevent spills. Place the sheet on the center rack of the oven, and bake for 15 minutes.

4 Finish the ramekins.

Top each ramekin with 1 tablespoon of the guacamole, and garnish with the chopped cilantro. Serve hot, 2 ramekins per person.

caponata and smoked gouda
mini-casseroles

The tart taste of caponata, now available at many grocery stores, is a stunning, salty foil to smoky, rich Gouda. These mini-casseroles deliver lots of flavor and are pretty to look at.

1 (16-ounce) tube ready-cooked polenta, sliced into 16 (½-inch-thick) medallions

1 (10-ounce) package cooked chicken (use cooked carved chicken breast)

1 (10-ounce) jar caponata (see note)

1 cup grated smoked Gouda

½ cup chopped fresh parsley

makes 4 servings
time: 25 minutes

1 Preheat the oven to 425° F.

2 Make the casseroles.
Spray 8 (12-ounce) ramekins with cooking spray. In each one, layer 1 polenta medallion, ¼ cup of the chicken, 2 tablespoons of the caponata, 2 tablespoons of the smoked Gouda, a second polenta medallion, and 2 more tablespoons of the cheese.

3 Bake the ramekins.
Set the ramekins on a cookie sheet to prevent spills. Place it on the center rack of the oven, and cook until bubbly and hot, about 15 minutes.

4 Garnish and serve.
Finish the ramekins with chopped parsley, and serve hot, 2 per person.

note: Caponata is a pungent Mediterranean olive spread made from olives, capers, and Mediterranean anchovies.

black bean and goat cheese
polenta casseroles

In Guatemala the black bean vines grow up the corn stalks. Not surprisingly, their flavors complement each other perfectly. Goat cheese adds a wild, gamy flavor layer. You can substitute pinto bean dip for the black beans if you prefer.

1 (16-ounce) tube ready-cooked polenta, sliced into 16 (½-inch-thick) medallions

1 (11-ounce) package cooked carved chicken breast

1 (10-ounce) can or jar black bean dip

1 cup crumbled goat cheese

½ cup fresh or prepared salsa (for garnish)

makes 4 servings
time: 25 minutes

1 Preheat the oven to 425° F.

2 Make the casseroles.
Spray 8 (12-ounce) ramekins with cooking spray. In each one layer 1 polenta medallion, 2 tablespoons of the chicken, 2 tablespoons of the black bean dip, 1 tablespoon of the cheese, a second polenta medallion, and 2 more tablespoons of the cheese.

3 Bake the ramekins.
Set the ramekins on a cookie sheet to prevent spills. Place the sheet on the center rack of the oven, and cook until bubbly and hot, about 15 minutes.

4 Garnish and serve.
Finish each ramekin with 1 tablespoon of the salsa. Serve hot, 2 per person.

individual polenta lasagnas

Fresh mozzarella gives this classic an extra kick, and the breakfast sausage adds flavor without taking extra time. For a really interesting taste, substitute smoked mozzarella.

1 (1-pound) brown-and-serve breakfast sausage roll, thinly sliced

1 (16-ounce) tube ready-cooked polenta, sliced into 16 (½-inch-thick) medallions

1½ cups marinara sauce

1 cup grated mozzarella

makes 4 servings
time: 25 minutes

1 Preheat the oven to 425° F.

2 Cook the sausage.
In a skillet, cook the sausage slices until brown, about 3 minutes. Drain on paper towels.

3 Layer the ingredients in the ramekins.
Spray 8 (12-ounce) ramekins with cooking spray, and in each one layer 1 polenta medallion, a few slices of the browned sausage, 1 tablespoon of the marinara sauce, 1 tablespoon of the mozzarella cheese, a second polenta medallion, and 2 more tablespoons of the cheese.

4 Bake the ramekins.
Set the ramekins on a cookie sheet to prevent spills. Place the sheet on the center rack of the oven, and cook until bubbly and hot, about 15 minutes.

5 Garnish and serve.
Finish the ramekins with 1 tablespoon of marinara. Serve hot, 2 per person.

barbecued pork and mango
chutney mini-casseroles

Barbecued pork in a tub is in your future. Try it. The spicy flavor of pork contrasts in a most alluring way with the sweet mango chutney. Add the crunch of scallions for a voluptuous series of textures. You don't need a crystal ball to see how this recipe would work.

½ (16-ounce) tube of ready-cooked polenta, sliced into 8 (½-inch-thick) medallions

1 (1-pound) package ready-to-serve barbecued pork

8 dashes of Tabasco sauce

1 (8-ounce) jar mango chutney

4 scallions, chopped

½ cup chopped fresh cilantro leaves (for garnish)

makes 4 servings
time: 25 minutes

1 Preheat the oven to 425° F.

2 Make the casseroles.
Spray 8 (12-ounce) ramekins with cooking spray, and in each one layer 1 polenta medallion, ¼ cup of the barbecued pork, 1 shot of the Tabasco, and 1 tablespoon of the mango chutney.

3 Bake the ramekins.
Set the ramekins on a cookie sheet to prevent spills. Place the sheet on the center rack of the oven, and cook until hot and bubbly, about 15 minutes.

4 Garnish and serve.
Finish the ramekins with chopped scallions, and garnish with cilantro. Serve hot, 2 per person.

pesto chicken and polenta
mini-casseroles

Prepared pesto is a welcome addition to most grocery store deli sections. The nutty and herbal flavor of pesto can improve many dishes. Try a jot of it tossed with hot pasta, poured over a block of cream cheese, or smeared on toast. Yum!

1 (16-ounce) tube ready-cooked polenta,
  sliced into 16 ($\frac{1}{2}$-inch-thick) medallions

1 (11-ounce) package cooked carved chicken breast

$\frac{3}{4}$ cup prepared pesto

1 cup grated mozzarella

$\frac{1}{2}$ cup chopped roasted red peppers from a jar

makes 4 servings
time: 25 minutes

1 Preheat the oven to 425° F.

2 Prepare the casseroles.
Spray 8 (12-ounce) ramekins with cooking spray. In each, layer 1 polenta medallion, $\frac{1}{4}$ cup of the chicken, 1 to 2 tablespoons of the pesto, 1 tablespoon of the mozzarella, a second polenta medallion, and 2 more tablespoons of the cheese.

3 Bake the ramekins.
Set the ramekins on a cookie sheet to prevent spills. Place the sheet on the center rack of the oven, and cook until bubbly and hot, about 15 minutes.

4 Garnish and serve the ramekins.
Finish each ramekin with a generous pinch of the roasted red peppers, and serve hot, 2 per person.

ginger chicken and polenta
mini-casseroles

Wake up your taste buds with these casseroles made with fresh and pickled ginger. The combo guarantees both hot and spicy flavor notes.

4 tablespoons (½ stick) butter

1 teaspoon chopped fresh ginger

Juice of 1 lemon

10 ounces (2 cups) chopped cooked chicken (from rotisserie bird or left-over cooked chicken)

½ (16-ounce) tube ready-cooked polenta, sliced into 8 (½-inch-thick) medallions

Japanese-style pickled ginger (for garnish)

makes 4 servings
time: 25 minutes

1 Preheat the oven to 425° F.

2 Season the chicken.
In a medium bowl, melt the butter in the microwave on HIGH (100 percent power) for 1 minute. Stir in the ginger, lemon juice, and the chopped chicken.

3 Make the casseroles.
Spray 8 (12-inch) ramekins with cooking spray. In each one layer 1 polenta medallion and one eighth of the chicken mixture.

4 Bake the ramekins.
Set the ramekins on a cookie sheet to prevent spills. Place the sheet on the center rack of the oven, and cook until hot, about 10 minutes.

5 Garnish and serve.
Finish the ramekins with a generous pinch of the pickled ginger. Serve hot, 2 ramekins apiece.

fresh pasta primer

Once the dairy case began to hold fresh stuffed pastas, home cooks had it made. Fresh pastas take less than half the time to cook than their dried counterparts. So fast to make you can stir together a little sauce from scratch. What is faster than boiling water? It's cooking a filled pasta in that boiling water while you stir together a little sauce. Kids like it. Adults will be amazed. Take your bow, Mom or Dad. This is truly prestidigitation.

1. Tortellini with Cilantro, Garlic, and Corn Dressing

2. Gorgonzola, Beets, and Toasted Walnuts with Meat Tortellini

3. Green Chile and Tomato Sausage Tortellini

4. Cheese Gnocchi with Butternut Squash and Raisins

tortellini with cilantro, garlic, and corn dressing

The Old World meets the New in this colorful dish that gives frozen corn a new lease on life.

4 garlic cloves, minced or pressed

¼ cup extra-virgin olive oil

3 tablespoons balsamic vinegar

1 teaspoon brown sugar

Salt and freshly milled pepper

2 cups (1 pound) pumpkin or cheese tortellini, fresh or frozen

1 bunch flat-leaf parsley, washed and stemmed

1 bunch cilantro, washed and stemmed

2 cups frozen corn, thawed*

4 cups mixed bitter greens (such as an Italian blend salad)

makes 4 servings
time: 15 minutes

1 Stir together the dressing.

Mix the garlic with the oil, vinegar, brown sugar, and salt and pepper to taste.

2 Cook the pasta.

Bring 6 quarts of water to a boil. Salt lightly; then add the tortellini and boil until tender, 10 to 12 minutes. Drain; then transfer to a large bowl. Pour the dressing over the pasta, and toss to coat.

3 Mix the vegetables.

In a large bowl, combine the parsley, cilantro, and corn, and toss to mix. Arrange about ½ cup bitter greens on each of 4 salad plates; then top each with the parsley mixture. Add about one quarter of the tortellini to each plate, drizzle some of the dressing over the greens, and serve.

* Set the corn on the countertop before you cook the pasta. It will thaw just enough to give you a cold, crisp salad ingredient.

gorgonzola, beets, and toasted walnuts with meat tortellini

Other than cooking the pasta, this dish is a real throw-together. Canned beets and Gorgonzola adore one another, and the beets turn the pasta a lovely pink color.

2 tablespoons salt

1 (9-ounce) package sausage or beef tortellini

1 (15-ounce can) sliced beets, drained and cut into small pieces

½ cup toasted walnuts

½ cup raisins

1 ounce Gorgonzola, crumbled

makes 4 servings
time: 10 minutes

1 Cook the pasta.

In a large stockpot, combine 6 quarts of water and the salt, and bring to a boil over high heat. Stir the tortellini into the boiling water, and cook for 8 to 10 minutes, or according to the instructions on the package.

2 Combine the ingredients.

Stir together the beets, walnuts, and raisins in the serving bowl.

3 Finish the dish.

Drain the cooked tortellini, and toss it with the beet mixture. Top with the cheese.

tip: Toasting intensifies the flavor of all nuts. We use the toaster oven set to the light toast setting.

green chile and tomato
sausage tortellini

All these ingredients can be kept in the pantry to give a basic vodka sauce a Latin twist.

2 tablespoons salt

1 pound fresh sausage tortellini

makes 6 servings
time: 25 minutes

Sauce

2 tablespoons butter

2 tablespoons olive oil

1/2 teaspoon hot red pepper flakes

1 (16-ounce) can tomatoes

1/2 (4.5-ounce) chopped green chiles

1/2 cup vodka

1 cup heavy cream

1 cup freshly grated Parmesan cheese

Salt and freshly milled pepper

1 Start the water boiling.
In a large stockpot, combine 6 quarts of water and the salt, and bring to a boil over high heat.

2 Make the sauce.
In a large skillet, heat the butter and oil together. Add the red pepper flakes, and cook for about 15 seconds. Add the tomatoes, chiles, and vodka, bring to a boil, and cook for 15 minutes. Add the cream and Parmesan cheese, and simmer for 5 more minutes. Taste, and adjust the seasonings with salt and pepper.

3 Cook the pasta.
Add the tortellini to the boiling water, and cook for 8 to 10 minutes, or according to the instructions on the package.

4 Combine and serve.
Toss the tortellini and the sauce in a large serving bowl or platter, and serve at once.

cheese gnocchi with butternut squash and raisins

Cheese gnocchi is such comfort food. It's now readily available frozen or in the fresh deli section at better grocery stores. And best of all, it cooks in one minute. Combined with frozen butternut squash and raisins, it's right off the menu of a trendy trattoria. Mangia!

2 tablespoons salt

2 tablespoons olive oil

1 garlic clove, minced

1 pound frozen butternut squash, thawed and drained

4 tablespoons (½ stick) butter

½ cup raisins

1 pound cheese gnocchi

Salt and freshly milled pepper

Parmesan cheese (for sprinkling)

makes 4 servings
time: 20 minutes

1 Start the water boiling.
Combine 6 quarts of water and the salt in a large stockpot, and bring to a boil over high heat.

2 Make the butternut squash mixture.
Coat a large skillet with the olive oil. Heat the skillet over high heat for 1 minute, and add the garlic and butternut squash. Reduce the heat to medium, and sauté until the squash is just starting to turn brown, 5 to 7 minutes. The squash will break down and become stringy and soft. Add the butter and raisins, and stir until the butter is melted.

3 Cook the gnocchi.
Add the gnocchi to the boiling water, and cook for 1 minute, or according to the package directions; time will vary depending on whether it is fresh or frozen.

4 Finish the dish.
Drain the gnocchi, and toss it with the butternut squash mixture. Taste, and add salt and pepper as needed. Sprinkle with Parmesan, and serve at once.

chapter three *
incredible frozen veggies

We Americans were dazzled by frozen foods about the time the Beaver began to ask Wally about the facts of life. Most of us have thawed, reheated, and regretted more frozen meals than we'd like to admit.

So when we started perusing the frozen food case, it was with a jaundiced eye. In our former lives as food snobs, we would never have admitted to more than frozen peas and corn in our home freezers. Well, maybe some ice cream, but you see where this is going.

Things have changed. We've gotten busier. Frozen foods have gotten better. We've given in to the magic. We are especially enamored of frozen creamed spinach and frozen mashed potatoes, two products that are the basis of extraordinary feats of kitchen prestidigitation.

And this section is one place where we have developed distinct brand loyalty. We are on our knees to Ore-Ida for all its great frozen potato products. (One of us loves the mashed potatoes; the other secretly craves the Tater Tots. No, we will not tell you which one.)

veggie starters

There are lots of times when you're willing to invest some time in a knockout entrée, but if you're like us, you may run out of gas when it comes to those first-impression makers: appetizers and hors d'oeuvres. Fortunately, help is no farther away than the vegetable section of the frozen food aisle, as these almost impossibly speedy starters demonstrate. Any one of them can be thrown together while your carbonnade simmers or your goose roasts. (And if you want to follow up with a rotisserie chicken for a half-scratch one-two punch, it's okay by us.)

1. **Mint, Spinach, and Pea Soup**

2. **Black-Eyed Peas with a Red-Pepper Vinaigrette**

3. **Crab, Artichoke, and Spinach Dip**

4. **Curried Spinach Dip**

5. **Warm Spinach-Parmesan Dip**

mint, spinach, and pea soup

This soup, made almost entirely of items plucked from the freezer section, is unbelievably rich and brightly flavored.

2 medium onions, chopped
(1 cup frozen chopped onions)

4 tablespoons (½ stick) butter

1 (10-ounce) box frozen spinach, thawed

1 (10-ounce) box frozen peas, thawed

½ bunch fresh mint leaves (about 2 cups loosely packed) (plus a few for garnish)

2 (13-ounce) cans chicken broth

1 cup heavy cream

Freshly milled pepper

makes 4 to 6 servings
time: 15 minutes

1 Sauté the onions.
In a medium saucepan over medium heat, cook the onions in the butter until they are translucent, about 5 minutes.

2 Add the other ingredients.
Stir in the spinach, peas, mint, chicken broth, and cream, and bring to a boil. Remove from the heat.

3 Purée the soup.
When the soup cools, purée it in a food processor or blender. If you desire a thinner soup, just add more chicken broth. Season with pepper to taste.

4 Serve.
Ladle into individual bowls, and garnish with a mint leaf. Serve hot or cold.

black-eyed peas with a red-pepper vinaigrette

Heaven knows that fresh black-eyed peas are good. We have discovered that with a bit of doctoring, the frozen ones are also great. This salad is wonderful warm or at room temperature alongside a slice of ham or chicken. Fresh thyme, finely chopped, really makes a difference here.

4 cups (1 quart) water

1 teaspoon salt

2 whole cloves

2 garlic cloves, chopped

2 bay leaves

1 tablespoon chopped fresh thyme (1 teaspoon dried)

1 (1-pound) bag frozen black-eyed peas

Vinaigrette

3 tablespoons red wine vinegar

2 tablespoons minced onion

1 tablespoon finely chopped fresh thyme (1 teaspoon dried)

2 peeled and diced red peppers*

$\frac{1}{4}$ cup olive oil

Salt and freshly milled pepper

*makes 6 to 8 servings
time: 25 minutes*

1 Cook the beans.

In a medium saucepan, bring the water, salt, cloves, garlic, bay leaves, and thyme to a boil. Add the black-eyed peas, and cook, uncovered, over medium heat until tender, about 15 minutes.

2 Make the vinaigrette.

Meanwhile, in the serving bowl, mix the vinegar, onion, thyme, and peppers. Stirring constantly, drizzle in the oil.

3 Finish the dish.

Drain the cooked peas, and discard the bay leaves. Toss the black-eyed peas with the vinaigrette. Taste, and adjust the seasoning with the salt and pepper. You can serve this dish immediately or chill it first.

* A French technique, peeling red peppers, is optional, but it really improves this dish. You get the crunch of a pepper without a tough skin.

crab, artichoke, and
spinach dip

This rich dip is a wonderful way to begin a meal. Serve it with a good bottle of dry white wine. Delicious.

2 tablespoons extra-virgin olive oil

2 garlic cloves, finely chopped

1 (10- or 11-ounce) package frozen creamed spinach, thawed*

¼ cup dry white wine

1 (6½-ounce) jar marinated artichoke hearts, drained

1 tablespoon fresh tarragon (for a different effect use 1 teaspoon dried tarragon or 1 tablespoon fresh dill)

½ pound fresh lump crabmeat, picked over for shells and cartilage

Juice and grated zest of ½ lemon

Tabasco sauce

makes 6 servings
time: 15 minutes

1 Sauté the garlic and spinach.

Remove the blade from a food processor bowl, and combine the olive oil, garlic, and creamed spinach in the bowl. Microwave on HIGH (100 percent power) for 4 minutes.

2 Combine the ingredients.

Remove the bowl from the microwave, and fit it with the steel blade. Add the white wine, artichoke hearts, and tarragon, and process until smooth. Add the crabmeat, lemon juice and zest, and Tabasco to taste, and pulse once or twice. Remove the blade, and return the bowl to the microwave. Cook on high for 4 more minutes.

3 Finish the dip.

Taste, and adjust the seasonings. Serve warm or at room temperature with crostini or toasted baguette slices.

* The spinach thaws best in the microwave on HIGH (100 percent power) for 2 minutes. We prefer Boston Market brand.

curried spinach dip

As Indian dishes prove, the spicy flavor of curry and the bitter edge of spinach are perfect partners. Here they are mellowed by cream sauce for a most elegant dip for crudités or crackers.

2 tablespoons extra-virgin olive oil

2 garlic cloves, finely chopped

1/2 teaspoon Madras curry powder

1/4 teaspoon ground cumin

1 (10- or 11-ounce) package frozen creamed spinach, thawed*

Pinch of cayenne

makes 6 servings
time: 10 minutes

1 Sauté the spices.

In a medium glass bowl, combine the olive oil, garlic, curry powder, and cumin. Heat in the microwave on HIGH (100 percent power) for 1 minute.

2 Mix in the spinach.

Add the creamed spinach and cayenne to the curry mixture, and microwave on HIGH for 2 minutes. Remove from the microwave, and stir thoroughly.

3 Finish the dip.

Taste, adjust the cayenne, and return to the microwave oven. Cook on HIGH for 3 more minutes, stirring halfway through. Serve warm with toasted pita triangles.

* The spinach thaws best in the microwave on HIGH (100 percent power) for 2 minutes. We prefer Boston Market brand.

warm spinach-parmesan dip

This warm dip is a company pleaser. It might be the ultimate in comfort food. Never admit to starting with frozen creamed spinach. If you don't volunteer the info, no one will be the wiser.

2 tablespoons extra-virgin olive oil

2 garlic cloves, finely chopped

1 (11-ounce) package frozen creamed spinach, thawed*

Juice and zest of ½ lemon

¼ teaspoon cayenne

1 cup grated fresh Parmesan (5-ounce wedge grated in the food processor with a micro plane)

makes 6 servings
time: 6 minutes

1 Season the spinach.

In a medium-large glass bowl, combine the olive oil and garlic. Microwave on HIGH (100 percent power) for 1 minute.

2 Combine the ingredients.

Add the creamed spinach, lemon juice and zest, and cayenne to the garlic mixture. Return to the microwave, and cook on HIGH for 4 minutes. Remove from the microwave, and stir thoroughly.

3 Finish the dip.

Stir the Parmesan into the spinach mixture, and return the bowl to the microwave. Cook on HIGH for 3 more minutes, stirring halfway through. This dip will begin to firm up as it cools. Serve warm with crostini or toasted baguette slices.

* The spinach thaws best in the microwave on HIGH (100 percent power) for 2 minutes. We prefer Boston Market brand.

fantastic vegetable sides

What most becomes a half-scratch entrée? Why, a half-scratch side, of course. Reach into your freezer for a bag of frozen something, wave your wand, and voilà: almost-instant elegance. So if you want to spend your afternoon at the farmer's market, be our guest. Rather spend the day someplace else? That's okay, too.

1. **Green Beans with Mustard Seeds and Toasted Coconut**

2. **Lemon-Garlic Broccoli**

3. **Lime and Garlic Spinach**

4. **Orzo with Creamed Spinach**

5. **Oven-Roasted Butternut Squash and Cumin Seed**

6. **Roasted Zucchini, Tomatoes, and Olives**

green beans with mustard seeds and toasted coconut

Sweetened coconut and mustard seed give dull old green beans an Indian flair. No one ever has to know that they started life as a frozen block.

2 tablespoons extra-virgin olive oil

½ teaspoon mustard seeds

3 tablespoons coconut flakes

1 (9-ounce) box frozen French-style green beans, thawed*

1 tablespoon butter

makes 4 servings
time: 15 minutes

1 Toast the mustard seeds and coconut.
Coat the bottom of a large skillet with olive oil. Heat over medium-high heat for 1 minute. Add the mustard seeds and half the coconut, and cook for 1 minute.

2 Sauté the beans.
Stir in the beans, and sauté for 3 to 5 minutes, until the beans are thoroughly heated. Stir in the butter. Divide onto the plates or in the center of a serving dish, and sprinkle with the remaining coconut. Serve at once.

* Best done under running warm water.

lemon-garlic broccoli

Broccoli is one of the more stable vegetables, but it can get boring. Roasted-garlic-flavored chicken broth in a can to the rescue. It gives any steamed vegetable a richer flavor. We've quit dreading broccoli. Honest!

1 (15-ounce) can roasted garlic chicken broth

2 teaspoons lemon zest

1 head broccoli, stems peeled and cut into bite-size pieces, florets broken into small pieces

Freshly milled pepper

makes 4 servings
time: 10 minutes

1 Prepare the broth.
Stir the broth and lemon zest together in a pot over high heat, and bring to a boil, about 5 minutes.

2 Cook the broccoli.
Add the broccoli to the pot, and cook for 3 to 5 minutes, until the broccoli is fork-tender. Sprinkle with the pepper to taste.

3 Serve.
Lift the broccoli from the pan using a slotted spoon, and serve at once.

lime and garlic spinach

Lime and garlic improve the flavor of most anything. Use it here in combination with a little chicken broth to bring out the best qualities of spinach. Popeye would go nuts.

3 tablespoons olive oil

2 garlic cloves, finely chopped

1 (16-ounce) bag frozen spinach, thawed

Juice and zest of 1 lime

½ cup chicken broth

Salt and freshly milled pepper

2 tablespoons butter

makes 4 servings
time: 6 minutes

1 Combine the vegetables.

In the bottom of a medium glass mixing bowl, stir together the olive oil and the chopped garlic. Microwave on HIGH (100 percent power) for 2 minutes. Remove from the microwave, and stir in the spinach, lime juice and zest, chicken broth, and salt and pepper to taste.

2 Finish the dish.

Return the dish to the microwave, and cook on HIGH for 5 minutes. Remove from the oven, and stir in the butter. Serve warm.

orzo with creamed spinach

Orzo is a small, shaped pasta that looks like big grains of rice but has the advantage of being cooked in seven minutes. Frozen spinach and dried orzo make a wonderful side to many main dishes.

4 cups chicken broth

2 cups (12 ounces) uncooked orzo

2 tablespoons butter

1 garlic clove, finely chopped

1 (10-ounce) package frozen creamed spinach

3 tablespoons Parmesan cheese

3 tablespoons pine nuts, toasted

makes 8 servings
time: 15 minutes

1 Cook the pasta.

In a medium saucepan over high heat, bring the chicken broth to a rolling boil. Add the orzo, and cook for 7 minutes, or just until al dente.

2 Combine the spinach and seasoning.

Meanwhile, in the serving bowl, combine the butter and garlic, and microwave on HIGH (100 percent power) for 1 minute. Add the frozen spinach, and microwave on HIGH for 5 more minutes.

3 Finish the dish.

Toss the cooked orzo with the spinach; then add the Parmesan. Top with the toasted pine nuts. Serve at once.

tip: Toasting intensifies the flavor of all nuts. We use the toaster oven set to the light toast setting.

oven-roasted butternut squash and cumin seed

Inspired by great Indian cooks we know, we select butternut squash and cumin as great complements to each other. With just a few spices, this otherwise bland frozen veggie can be vastly improved.

3 tablespoons extra-virgin olive oil

3 garlic cloves, chopped

$\frac{1}{2}$ teaspoon cumin seed

1 (1-pound) bag frozen butternut squash, thawed*

2 tablespoons butter

Salt and freshly milled pepper

makes 4 servings
time: 20 minutes

1 Preheat the oven to 400° F.

2 Sauté the garlic.

In the bottom of a 8 × 11½ × 2-inch glass or ceramic baking dish, stir together the olive oil, garlic, and cumin seed. Microwave on HIGH (100 percent power) for 2 minutes. Toss in the squash, and thoroughly mix all the ingredients.

3 Roast the squash.

Place the baking dish on the center oven rack, and roast for 7 minutes. Remove from the oven, stir in the butter, and roast for 4 more minutes. Season to taste with the salt and pepper. Serve warm.

* Zap the squash in the microwave for 1 minute to thaw.

roasted zucchini, tomatoes, and olives

Who says you have to boil frozen vegetables? Roasting concentrates the flavors nicely. This classic provides a quick side on nights when you can't cope with prepping veggies.

3 tablespoons extra-virgin olive oil

2 garlic cloves, finely chopped

1 (14.5-ounce) can tomatoes, drained and chopped

1 (16-ounce) bag frozen zucchini, thawed*

1/2 cup chopped pitted black olives

Juice and zest of 1 lemon

Salt and freshly milled pepper

*makes 4 servings
time: 20 minutes*

1 Preheat the oven to 400° F.

2 Combine the ingredients.
In the bottom of an 8 × 11^1/$_2$ × 2-inch glass or ceramic baking dish, stir together 2 tablespoons of the olive oil and the garlic. Microwave on HIGH (100 percent power) for 2 minutes. Remove from the microwave, and toss in the tomatoes, zucchini, black olives, and lemon juice and zest. Thoroughly mix all the ingredients.

3 Roast the vegetables.
Place the mixture on the center rack of the oven, and roast for 15 minutes. Season with salt and pepper to taste. Serve warm.

* Best done in the microwave on high (100 percent power) for 2 minutes right in the bag.

potato main courses to mystify

As cooks, we never thought we would see the day when frozen or refrigerated mashed potatoes would have a place in our grocery carts. But they bear no relation to dried spuds in a box. The timesaving advantages of not having to peel and boil potatoes are spectacular. Call them smashed potatoes or potato purée instead of mashed potatoes, and you have a four-star restaurant accompaniment—minus the aching hands and time spent prepping the spuds!

1. **Shepherd's Pie with Roasted Red Pepper and Roast Beef**

2. **Saffron Garlic Potato Purée with Ham Strip Topping**

3. **All-in-One Sunday Supper with Glazed Shallot Mashed Potatoes**

4. **Cashew Fish *en Papillote***

5. **Belize Fish Fillets on Wasabi Mashed Potatoes**

6. **Spanish Tortilla**

7. **Italian Peppers, Potatoes, and Sausage on a Roll**

8. **Beef Tenderloin Steaks with Potatoes and Dill-Mustard Sauce**

shepherd's pie with roasted
red pepper and roast beef

There isn't a man alive who doesn't cheer up at the sight of shepherd's pie on his plate. Don't tell him it took about 5 minutes to throw together. This isn't cooking; it's assembling.

4 cups prepared frozen mashed potatoes

1 pound thinly sliced deli roast beef, cut into bite-size pieces

1 (½ pint) jar roasted red pepper pesto (sometimes called red pepper sauce—Contadina makes a great one)

Salt and freshly milled pepper

makes 4 servings
time: 25 minutes

1 **Preheat the oven to 350° F.**

2 **Make the pie.**
Spritz a 2-quart casserole dish or Pyrex bowl with cooking spray, and spread the mashed potatoes in the bottom. Top with a layer of roast beef pieces, and then a layer of the red pepper pesto. Season to taste with salt and pepper.

3 **Bake and serve.**
Place the dish on the center rack of the oven, and cook for 15 to 20 minutes. Serve hot.

saffron garlic potato purée with ham strip topping

Saffron lightly perfumes and brightly colors any dish that it is added to. Keep these pricey but versatile threads on hand to spruce up potatoes, rice, and even couscous.

2 tablespoons extra-virgin olive oil

2 tablespoons butter

½ teaspoon saffron threads

1 garlic clove, minced

1 cup milk

2 cups frozen mashed potatoes

2 cups fully cooked ham cut into bite-size strips

makes 4 servings
time: 15 minutes

1 Sauté the saffron and garlic.

In a large glass bowl, combine the olive oil, butter, saffron threads, garlic, and milk, and microwave on HIGH (100 percent power) for 4 minutes.

2 Cook the potatoes.

Stir in the potatoes, and cook for 5 minutes. Stir; then cook for 5 more minutes. Stir again.

3 Build the dish.

Top with ham strips, and run it under the broiler to brown, about 5 minutes.

all-in-one sunday supper with glazed shallot mashed potatoes

Did you know that if you preheat a big ovenproof skillet on top of the stove while you're preheating the oven, you could roast a cut-up chicken in thirty minutes? You'll get everything—crisp, glistening mahogany skin and tender, moist meat. Slap those chicken pieces into the hot pan, then into the blast furnace of a hot oven. Meanwhile, you can tart up some ready-made potatoes by sizzling a shallot in butter along with frozen peas and pearl onions. Add potatoes and milk. Has Sunday dinner ever been easier?

1 cut-up chicken (3 to 4 pounds)

Salt and cracked black pepper

2 tablespoons olive oil

1 lemon, cut in half

makes 4 servings
time: 40 minutes or less

Glazed Shallot Mashed Potatoes

2 tablespoons butter

1 shallot, minced

$1/3$ cup frozen peas

$1/3$ cup frozen pearl onions (optional)

$2^2/3$ cups frozen mashed potatoes

$1^1/3$ cups milk

Salt and pepper

1 Prepare the chicken.

Heat the oven to 425°F. Season the chicken pieces thoroughly with salt and pepper.

2 Roast the chicken.

Heat a large (12- to 14-inch) ovenproof skillet until it smokes; then add the oil. Quickly add the chicken pieces, skin-side up, and carefully squeeze lemon juice over all of them. Place the skillet into the oven. Roast the bird for 30 minutes, or until the pieces run clear when the thigh is pierced with a knife tip.

3 Make the mashed potatoes.

About 5 minutes before the bird is done, heat the butter in a medium pan; then sizzle the shallots for 3 minutes. Add the peas and pearl onions, and cook for 1 minute longer. Now add the potatoes and milk, and stir with a fork for 2 to 3 minutes, or until smooth. Adjust the seasonings with salt and pepper. Serve alongside the chicken.

cashew fish *en papillote*

Of course you know what en papillote *means: "in a paper bag." Make this in a parchment package or a foil pouch. Either way, it makes dinner fast and foolproof with no—repeat, no—cleanup.*

2 fish steaks (such as shark, salmon, halibut, swordfish)

4 tablespoons soft butter (plus more for potatoes)

¼ cup chopped fresh parsley

3 garlic cloves

¼ cup salted cashews

2 cups frozen or refrigerated mashed potatoes

2 tablespoons wasabi powder

Salt and freshly milled pepper

makes 2 servings
time: 25 minutes

1 Prepare the fish for cooking.

Preheat the oven to 400°F. On a baking sheet, lay out two square pieces (10 × 10 inches) of parchment or aluminum foil. Spritz them with cooking spray and lay a fish steak on each one.

2 Make the cashew butter.

Combine the butter, parsley, garlic, and nuts in a food processor, and pulse to make a rough purée. Smear the butter mixture on all sides of the fish. Fold the top of the paper to form a bag, sealing the edges with triple folds.

3 Cook the fish.

Slide the baking sheet on the middle rack of the oven, and cook until the fish is done and the bag begins to puff up a bit, about 15 minutes. Serve from the bag directly onto the dinner plate, opening the bag in front of the diner.

4 Make the mashed potatoes.

Following package directions, heat the mashed potatoes, seasoning them with wasabi that's been moistened with water. (Use more or less wasabi as you prefer.) Finish flavoring to taste with salt and pepper and butter.

belize fish fillets on wasabi mashed potatoes

Our friend Meredith Pollak, one of the rare cooks who tries something new every night, first tasted this dish in a Belize restaurant. When she inquired of the chef, she learned that the secret was mayonnaise. We use our new favorite—frozen mashed potatoes punched up with a shot of wasabi—as mouthwatering base for the fish. All you need to complete this dinner is a glass of substantial red wine— perhaps a good pinot noir—and a piece of crusty bread.

Olive oil

1 yellow onion, thinly sliced

½ bell pepper, thinly sliced (or jarred roasted red peppers)

1 tomato, thinly sliced

¾ pound fresh or frozen fish fillets (we used salmon)

2 tablespoons drained capers

3 tablespoons mayonnaise

Salt and pepper

2⅔ cups frozen mashed potatoes

1⅓ cups milk

2 tablespoons wasabi powder, or to taste

Butter

makes 2 servings
time: 25 minutes

1 Assemble and bake the fish.

Preheat the oven to 350°F. Coat a baking dish with a tight-fitting lid with olive oil. Layer in half the onion, pepper, and tomato slices. Slather both sides of the fish fillets with mayo, and place in the baking dish. Top with the remaining vegetables and the capers. Season with the salt and pepper. Bake, covered, for about 20 minutes, until the fish flakes.

2 Make the mashed potatoes.

Meanwhile, stir together the potatoes and milk. Cook and stir until they are smooth. Dissolve the wasabi powder in water; stir it into the potatoes. Taste, and adjust the flavorings with additional wasabi. Add a shot of butter to taste.

3 Serve.

Place a serving of potatoes on 2 warmed dinner plates; top with the fish and vegetables.

spanish tortilla

We love it when old-world cooks give fancy names to simple dishes. Call it an omelet, a frittata—it's supper in a pan for two, or a little plate for six unexpected guests. Use those handy 80-percent-cooked potatoes to start, and the job just got easier. Serve it hot in about twenty-five minutes, or at room temperature.

2 tablespoons olive oil

1 (10-ounce) package fresh or frozen garlic Idaho potatoes

1 cup fresh or frozen chopped onions

Salt, black pepper, and cayenne

2 teaspoons butter

6 eggs, whisked to a froth

makes 2 dinner servings
or 6 appetizers
time: 25 minutes

1 Sauté the vegetables.

In a medium ovenproof skillet, heat the oil; then cook the potatoes and onions over medium heat, seasoning to taste with salt, pepper, and cayenne. Stir often, and cook until the potatoes are tender and beginning to brown, about 5 minutes. Preheat the broiler.

2 Cook the eggs.

Add the butter to the pan, melt, and then pour in the eggs. Reduce the heat to low, and continue to cook until all but the top is cooked. Run the tortilla under the broiler to brown for 2 minutes.

3 Serve.

Loosen the edges with a knife, and slide the tortilla onto a serving plate. Slice it into wedges: fat ones for 2, skinny ones for a crowd. Add a side of sliced tomatoes, some great toast, and maybe some mixed olives.

italian peppers, potatoes, and sausage on a roll

A staple of Italian street fairs everywhere, this traditional Italian favorite can be served on a plate or inside a roll. Cook it on a grill or in a skillet. Use best quality fully-cooked sausage—we like Bruce Aidells's low-fat Chicken & Apple tossed with bell peppers and 80-percent-precooked roasted Idaho potatoes. It's magic that needs only a great roll and bottle of red to complete it.

¼ cup extra-virgin olive oil

4 to 6 fully cooked sausages, split lengthwise

1 red, yellow, or green bell pepper, cut into strips

1 (10-ounce) package frozen garlic parmesan sauté-ready potatoes

1 tablespoon drained capers

1 cup grape or cherry tomatoes

4 hero rolls or hot dog buns

makes 4 servings
time: 15 minutes

1 Cook the sausages.

Heat a large skillet over medium-high heat. Coat it with some of the oil, and then fry the sausages until they're nearly brown, about 5 minutes.

2 Cook the vegetables.

Add the bell peppers, potatoes, and the seasoning mix from the potatoes to a bowl. Toss with the remaining oil; then pour into the skillet with the sausages. Cook and stir until the potatoes and peppers are brown, about 5 minutes. Add the capers and tomatoes, and heat through.

3 Fill the sandwiches.

Split the rolls, and heat them on the grill or in a toaster oven. Pile the sausage mixture into rolls.

beef tenderloin steaks
with potatoes and dill-mustard sauce

Mustard really pumps up the flavor of the classic meat-and-potatoes combo here. Serve a great piece of beef, and you've got a carnivore's dream without breaking a sweat.

2 tablespoons olive oil, plus more for rubbing steaks

1 medium yellow onion, thinly sliced

¼ cup grainy or Dijon mustard

½ cup chicken broth

2 (10-ounce) containers sliced frozen red potatoes (we like Boston Market) with garlic and dill, thawed*

Salt and freshly milled pepper

4 beef tenderloin steaks, 2 to 3 inches thick

2 tablespoons vegetable oil

Fresh parsley, chopped (for garnish)

makes 4 servings
time: 25 minutes

1 Preheat the oven to 400° F.

2 Make the potato base.
In the bottom of a 13 × 9 × 2-inch baking dish, stir together the olive oil and onion. Cook in the microwave on HIGH (100 percent power) for 3 minutes. Stir in the mustard, chicken broth, and potatoes. Return to the microwave, and cook on HIGH for 7 more minutes. Taste and adjust seasoning with the salt and pepper.

3 Prepare the steaks.
Rub the steaks with the olive oil, salt, and pepper.

4 Sear the steaks.

Heat a medium skillet dry on high heat for 2 minutes. Reduce the heat to medium-high, add the vegetable oil, and sear the steaks for 2 minutes per side in batches so as not to crowd the pan. Sear the sides, as well. The steaks will be golden brown on the outside and rare on the inside. The steaks will finish cooking in the oven. Hold them on a plate.

5 Assemble the dish.

Top the potato mixture with the seared steaks, and place on the center rack of the oven. Cook for 15 minutes to preferred doneness. The internal temperature of the steaks should read about 130° to 135°F for medium rare.

6 Serve.

Garnish with the chopped parsley, and serve warm.

✻ Best done in the microwave for 5 minutes for 2 containers

part two

secrets of the pantry shelf

If we've said it once, we've said it a thousand times: a half-scratch magician is only as good as his or her pantry. We're not talking dry pasta with canned sauce here—many of the recipes in this section use fresh ingredients, too. But a well-stocked pantry means you can turn a stop at the deli, a dash through the express lane for some steaks or chops, or a quick trip to the greengrocer into dinner—*now.* And if you've been paying attention, you're already stocked up on ready-to-eat chicken carvers, beef crumbles, or whatever protein makes your crowd happiest. So break out that can opener; it's dinnertime!

chapter four *
opening can illusions

Food has come in cans for a full century. But while canning technology was hailed as a breakthrough when it was first introduced, we, like many of our cohorts, turned our noses up at canned provisions in the eat-fresh-or-die decade known as the 1990s. Now, we've come down off that high horse and recognized there are plenty of products that come in a can that can be transformed into savory, nutritious meals in less than the blink of an eye. And we'll take that any night of the week, food snobs be damned.

About the only caveat to using cans is to remember that most canned goods are way salty. When using any canned product, be sure to taste the food before salting it at *all*. You're importing a lot of salt, and in many cases, it will be plenty for the finished dish. You'll find we say "season with salt and pepper to taste" a lot in this section because we want to encourage you to use judgment and think before you start adding salt to a dish that may have started with tablespoons of the same via the salted canned good.

Remember, too, that lots of "canned goods" actually come in jars. Mushrooms, beets, and roasted peppers come to mind. Yes, you can buy them in a can, but we usually choose those gorgeous glass jars. Just seeing that glistening jar of ruby beets when we open the pantry makes us happy.

Canned goods come to the rescue in sauce-making, too. In the Asian tropics, where refrigeration isn't always available, coconut milk is the liquid of choice for making smooth, silky sauces and soups. Does a recipe call for cream and you're out? Try substituting coconut milk. You will be pleasantly surprised at the added interest in taste that results. We've offered you one coconut milk sauce that can be used interchangeably with chicken, fish, or shrimp—just like they do in the Thai restaurant down the block. Keep canned coconut milk on hand. It's one of the real half-scratch magicians' tricks.

A lot of things we do with cans and jars don't even require recipes. Remember, you can always pop open a container of such gorgeous prepared items as onions, mushrooms, or beets and serve them forth. They'll add just the right fillip to an ordinary after-work dinner. Who knew it could be so easy?

beans and more

Canned beans have probably been the basis of more half-scratch meals than any other item in our pantries. From quick hors d'oeuvres to hearty main course salads and beds for pan-grilled meats, they're ready when you are. Just be sure to rinse them well before using and add salt judiciously. You'll also find uses here for canned beets, canned corn, and more!

1. White-Bean and Sage Bruschetta

2. Chickpea, Garlic, and Parsley Spread

3. Spicy Red-Bean Spread

4. Clam Up for Company Spread

5. Chicken Confetti Salad

6. Corn and Black Bean Salad

7. Red Pepper, Chickpeas, Parsley, and Lemon Salad

8. Beets in Orange Vinaigrette on a Bed of Baby Greens

9. Black-Olive Salad with Chopped Celery

10. Courtney's Thanksgiving Creamed Onions

11. Three-Bean Skillet Supper with Kielbasa

12. Fast Pasta Fagioli

13. Chili-Rubbed Steaks on Black Beans with
     Lime Cream

14. New York Minute Strip Steak on a Bed of
     Wilted Spinach and Chickpeas

15. Pan-Grilled Pork Chops on Corn and Red
     Pepper Chutney

16. Pan-Grilled Rosemary Lamb Chops on
     White Beans with Tomato

17. Pan-Grilled Veal Chops on Green Olive
     Coulis

18. Pan-Grilled Veal Chops on Marinated
     Mushrooms and Garlic

19. Sautéed Scallops in a Citrus-Curry Sauce

white-bean and sage
bruschetta

This warm hors d'oeuvre is rich without being too filling. Made from a can of beans, these are purely sleight of hand.

3 tablespoons extra-virgin olive oil

1 garlic clove, finely chopped

1 (15-ounce) can cannellini beans, rinsed and drained

2 tablespoons butter

3 to 5 fresh sage leaves, cut into thin strips

Toasts or sliced baguette brushed with olive oil and toasted

makes 4 to 6 servings
time: 10 minutes

1 Sauté the garlic.
Coat the bottom of the pan with the olive oil, and over medium heat sauté the garlic until it is just barely beginning to turn golden.

2 Cook the beans.
Stir in the drained and rinsed beans, and cook until the beans are warmed through, 3 to 5 minutes. Stir in the butter and the sage.

3 Make the bruschettas.
Spoon 1 to 2 teaspoons of the bean mixture onto each piece of toasted bread. Serve at once.

chickpea, garlic, and parsley spread

Canned chickpeas are among the top ten ingredients the half-scratch cook should always keep on hand. They are great in salads, and with the addition of some butter and cumin seed, you have an interesting side dish. Keep fresh parsley, too. Fresh herbs always spruce up dishes, and parsley is the standard. This dip is ready before you know it.

¼ cup extra-virgin olive oil

2 garlic cloves, finely chopped

1 (19-ounce) can chickpeas, rinsed and drained

½ cup fresh parsley leaves

Juice and grated zest of 1 lemon

Salt and freshly milled pepper

makes 6 servings
time: 6 minutes

1 Sauté the garlic.
Remove the blade from your food processor bowl; then combine the olive oil and garlic in the bowl. Heat in the microwave on HIGH (100 percent power) for 1 minute.

2 Purée the dip.
Return the bowl to the processor, and fit in the blade. Add the chickpeas, fresh parsley, lemon juice and zest, and salt and pepper to taste. Process until thoroughly mixed.

3 Season and serve.
Taste, and adjust the pepper and lemon juice. Serve at room temperature with toasted pita triangles.

spicy red-bean spread

For a truly magical appetizer, whiz up a can of drained kidney beans along with spices from your pantry, stir in sour cream, and you're ready to entertain. Don't have kidney beans? Substitute black beans or canned pintos. Make the spread and keep it up to a week, covered in the refrigerator.

1 medium onion, halved

3 garlic cloves

1 (16-ounce) can red kidney beans, rinsed and drained

1 roasted red pepper from a jar, drained

Juice and zest of 1 lemon (or lime)

1 teaspoon ground cumin

1 tablespoon chili powder

½ cup cilantro

1 cup sour cream

Salt and freshly milled pepper

makes 2 cups
time: 5 minutes or less

1 Make the spread.

Pulse the onion and garlic in a food processor to chop finely. Add the beans, red pepper, lemon juice and zest, cumin, and chili powder. Pulse to make a rough purée. Stir in the cilantro and sour cream, and pulse to combine. Adjust seasonings with salt and pepper.

2 Serve.

Cover and refrigerate until serving time. Serve from a decorative bowl surrounded by chips, crudités, or crackers.

clam up for company spread

Blend the briny flavor of clams with a touch of garlic and chives, and smooth it together with butter and cream cheese for a spread that's great for breadsticks, crudités, or dolloped onto a bowl of chowder.

2 (6½-ounce) cans minced clams, drained and juice reserved

1 garlic clove, minced

1 tablespoon fresh chives

¼ teaspoon Worcestershire sauce

Zest and 2 tablespoons juice of 1 lemon

¼ teaspoon low-sodium soy sauce

Shot of Tabasco

½ pound Philadelphia cream cheese, softened

2 tablespoons unsalted butter, at room temperature

makes 6 to 8 servings
time: 15 minutes or less

Make the dip.

In a medium, nonreactive bowl, stir together the clams, garlic, and chives. In a glass measure, combine the Worcestershire sauce, lemon zest and juice, 2 tablespoons of the reserved clam juice, soy, and Tabasco. Stir to mix; then pour over the clam mixture. Add the softened cream cheese and butter, and blend with a fork or in a food processor. Transfer to a decorative bowl, cover, and refrigerate until serving time.

chicken confetti salad

Quick and easy, this salad requires little of you beyond chopping a bell pepper. Don't have one? Use a roasted red pepper from a jar; then assemble the salad with the remaining ingredients. Make it and refrigerate for up to 2 hours before serving.

1 (15-ounce) can chickpeas, rinsed and drained

1 (15-ounce) can black beans, rinsed and drained

½ cup corn kernels (fresh, frozen, or canned)

½ cup frozen peas

1 red bell pepper, diced

2 scallions, diced

1 yellow crookneck squash, shredded

2 cups shredded roast chicken

1 head butter lettuce

Dressing

¼ cup rice vinegar

2 teaspoons Dijon mustard

½ teaspoon chili powder

Salt and pepper

¼ cup extra-virgin olive oil

makes 4 servings
time: 20 minutes or less

1 Assemble the salad.

Combine the chickpeas, beans, corn, peas, pepper, scallions, squash, and chicken in a large salad bowl. Toss to mix.

2 Combine with the dressing.

Pour the vinegar into a small jar with a tight-fitting lid; then whisk in the mustard, chili powder, and salt and pepper to taste. Add the oil, cover, and shake. Pour the dressing over the salad, and toss thoroughly. Cover and refrigerate for up to 8 hours.

3 Serve.

Make a bed of butter lettuce on 4 dinner plates. Divide the salad among the plates, and serve immediately.

corn and black bean salad

Canned corn and beans . . . always around, always great. If you give them a quick rinse and toss them with some crunchy vegetables, you have a great salad.

1 (15-ounce) can corn, rinsed and drained

1 (15-ounce) can black beans, rinsed and drained

½ red onion, chopped

½ red or green bell pepper, chopped

1 stalk celery, chopped

½ cup coarsely chopped cilantro leaves

½ cup fresh lemon juice

½ cup extra-virgin olive oil

½ teaspoon ground cumin

Salt and freshly milled pepper

makes 6 servings
time: 20 minutes

1 Make the salad.

In the serving bowl, toss the corn, black beans, red onion, bell pepper, celery, cilantro, lemon juice, olive oil, and cumin, and mix thoroughly. Taste, and add the salt and freshly milled pepper as needed.

2 Marinate.

Cover and refrigerate for 15 minutes, or until serving time.

red pepper, chickpeas, parsley, and lemon salad

Canned chickpeas are healthy, maintain their texture nicely, and can really improve any salad. They are great in a pinch.

1 red bell pepper, chopped

2 (14-ounce) cans chickpeas, rinsed and drained

½ yellow onion, finely chopped (about ¾ cup)

1 garlic clove, finely chopped

½ cup pitted black olives, coarsely chopped

½ cup fresh flat-leaf parsley, chopped

¼ cup extra-virgin olive oil

¼ cup fresh lemon juice

Grated zest of 1 lemon

¼ cup white wine vinegar

½ teaspoon salt

Freshly milled black pepper

makes 6 servings
time: 20 minutes

1 Make the salad.
Toss the red pepper, chickpeas, onion, garlic, olives, parsley, olive oil, lemon juice, zest, and vinegar. Taste, and adjust the seasonings with the salt and pepper.

2 Marinate.
Cover and chill for 15 minutes.

beets in orange vinaigrette
on a bed of baby greens

If you think you don't like beets, give them another try. These lovely little red jewels are a great alternative to broccoli on nights when you have no time, yet no patience for the run of the mill. A citrus vinaigrette brightens their flavor and cuts the sweetness. They're delicious straight from the container: hot, cold, or as is.

Orange Vinaigrette

makes 4 servings
time: 10 minutes

- 2 tablespoons white wine vinegar
- 2 tablespoons fresh orange juice
- Zest of 1 orange
- 1 teaspoon sugar
- ½ teaspoon salt
- 3 tablespoons extra-virgin olive oil

Salad

- 2 (15-ounce) cans or jars beets
- 4 cups baby greens

1 Mix the vinaigrette.

In the bottom of a medium bowl, use a fork or whisk to stir together the vinegar, orange juice, zest, sugar, and salt. Stirring constantly, add the olive oil in a thin stream until it emulsifies.

2 Marinate the beets.

Toss the beets with the vinaigrette. Cover and refrigerate until ready to serve over a bed of baby greens.

black-olive salad with
chopped celery

Canned black olives are cheap, versatile, and easy to keep on hand. The crunch of good old celery is a great textural complement to these black beauties.

2 tablespoons extra-virgin olive oil

2 tablespoons red wine vinegar

½ teaspoon freshly milled pepper

1 cup coarsely chopped celery

1 cup coarsely chopped pitted black olives

makes 4 servings
time: 5 minutes

Make the salad.

In the bottom of the serving bowl, mix the olive oil, vinegar, and pepper. Toss in the celery and olives. Refrigerate until ready to serve.

courtney's thanksgiving creamed onions

We would not have believed this if we hadn't seen it with our own eyes. On Thanksgiving Day, when the kitchen at our cousins Courtney and John Sjostrom's Philadelphia home was humming with activity, Courtney calmly pulled out a jar, a can, and a baking dish and proceeded to make her mother's holiday standby. Turkey never had it so good.

2 (13-ounce) cans cream of celery soup

2 (16-ounce) jars onions, drained

makes 6 to 8 servings
time: 20 minutes

Make the onions.

Preheat the oven to 350°F. Combine the soup and onions in a 2-quart casserole dish, and pop it into the oven for 20 minutes. You'll be amazed. It's that easy, and it tastes great beside that big bland bird.

three-bean skillet supper with kielbasa

Tater Tots, those bullets of flavor you remember from your wasted youth, work admirably atop a skillet supper made from nothing more than three cans of beans and a ring of sausage. This reheats well.

2 cups frozen potato nuggets
2 bacon slices, chopped
1 tablespoon olive oil
2 cups chopped onions
2 garlic cloves, smashed
1 cup chopped red or green bell pepper
1 pound kielbasa, cut into coins
1 (15-ounce) can chickpeas
1 (15-ounce) can red kidney beans
1 (15-ounce) can Italian green beans
$\frac{1}{4}$ cup packed brown sugar
$\frac{1}{2}$ cup ketchup
1 tablespoon red wine vinegar
1 tablespoon chili powder

makes 6 servings
time: 30 minutes

1 Bake the potato nuggets.

Preheat the oven to 450°F. Spritz a pie pan or cookie sheet with cooking spray, and arrange the nuggets, in a single layer. Bake until crisp, about 15 minutes.

2 Brown the onions and meat.

While the potatoes bake, heat a large skillet over medium-high heat. Add the bacon and olive oil, and cook until the bacon begins to crisp. Add the onions, then the garlic, cooking and stirring until the onion becomes translucent. Add the bell pepper and kielbasa. Stir to mix.

3 Make the sauce.

Pour the juices from the beans into a 2-cup measure; rinse and drain the beans. Stir the brown sugar, ketchup, vinegar, and chili powder into the bean liquid, and add to the pan with the onions and meat. Boil for about 10 minutes on high; add the drained beans. Cook until the sauce begins to thicken, about 15 minutes.

4 Serve.

Top the bean dish with crisp potato nuggets, and serve from the pan.

fast pasta fagioli

A classic everyday Italian favorite that combines pasta and white beans punched up with sage, rosemary, and garlic—count this as one of your private blessings. The original, of course, probably started with homemade pasta and dried beans—but hey, what are cans for? Everyone will eat this: kids, grandma, cranky Uncle Fred. All you need to complete the meal is a serving of salad out of a bag, and a loaf of crusty bread.

1 cup small dry pasta (fusilli, orecchiette, or broken linguine)

2 (16-ounce) cans cannellini beans, rinsed and drained

5 garlic cloves

2 sprigs fresh sage (1 teaspoon dried) (plus more for garnish)

1 sprig rosemary (1 tablespoon dried) (plus more for garnish)

1 (15-ounce) can chicken broth

1 (8-ounce) can tomato sauce

Salt and freshly milled black pepper

Extra-virgin olive oil (for garnish)

makes 4 servings
time: 20 minutes

1 Cook the pasta.

In a large pot, bring 4 quarts of water to a boil. Add the salt and then add pasta. Cook the pasta according to the package instructions. Drain.

2 Cook the beans.

Meanwhile, stir the beans with garlic, sage, rosemary, chicken broth, and tomato sauce in a large saucepan. Simmer while the pasta cooks. Pour the drained pasta into the beans. Cook and stir to heat through; adjust the seasonings with the salt and pepper.

3 Serve.

Ladle into soup bowls. Garnish with olive oil and extra sage or rosemary leaves.

chili-rubbed steaks on black beans with lime cream

Gebhardt's chili powder is the one we love, but find your own favorite. The combo of steak, sour cream, lime juice, and chili will make your mouth water.

2 tablespoons extra-virgin olive oil

1 garlic clove, chopped

2 tablespoons chili powder

2 tablespoons fresh lime juice

2 (15-ounce) cans black beans, rinsed and drained

4 New York strip steaks (also known as shell steaks)

Salt and freshly milled pepper

makes 4 servings
time: 25 minutes

Lime Cream

1 cup sour cream

3 tablespoons lime juice

1 teaspoon grated lime zest, chopped

Salt

½ cup crushed tortilla chips (for garnish)

1 Make the bean base.

In a medium glass bowl, stir together 1 tablespoon of the olive oil and the garlic. Microwave on HIGH (100 percent power) for 2 minutes. Stir in 1 tablespoon of the chili powder, 2 tablespoons of the lime juice, and the beans. Cook on HIGH for 3 more minutes.

2 Pan-grill the steaks.

Dry the steaks thoroughly, and rub with remaining tablespoon of chili powder. Heat a medium skillet on high heat for 2 minutes. Reduce the heat to medium-high, add the remaining tablespoon of oil, and cook the steaks for 3 to 5 minutes per side, or to desired level of doneness, 135° to 140°F for medium rare.

3 Make the lime cream.

Stir the sour cream, lime juice, and lime zest together in a small bowl with salt to taste.

4 Assemble the dish.

Arrange the steak slices on top of the cooked beans. Drizzle with the lime cream, and top with crushed tortilla chips. Serve warm.

new york minute strip steak
on a bed of wilted
spinach and chickpeas

It would take you longer to have a plate in front of you if you were to walk to your corner bistro and order a burger. And wouldn't you rather have this restaurant-style presentation of beef with bitter greens and beans?

4 New York strip steaks (also known as shell steaks)

2 tablespoons olive oil

Salt and freshly milled pepper

4 to 6 ounces blue cheese (Maytag, Stilton, or Gorgonzola)

3 tablespoons balsamic vinegar

1 (16-ounce) can chickpeas, rinsed and drained

1 (10-ounce) package tripled-washed baby spinach

makes 4 servings
time: 15 minutes

1 Preheat the skillet.
Place a dry skillet over medium-high heat for 2 to 3 minutes.

2 Prep the steaks.
Rub the steaks with 1 tablespoon of the olive oil and salt and pepper to taste.

3 Cook the steaks.
Add the remaining tablespoon of olive oil to the skillet, and heat for 1 more minute. Then cook the steaks for 3 to 4 minutes per side, until desired level of doneness. Remove the steaks to a warm plate, and top each steak with some of the blue cheese. The cheese will begin to melt.

4 Wilt the spinach.
Over medium-high heat add the vinegar and chickpeas and cook for 2 minutes. Turn off the heat, add the spinach, and toss thoroughly.

5 Assemble the dish.
Divide the spinach mixture among 4 plates, and top with the steak and blue cheese.

tip: Keep a good balsamic vinegar on hand at all times. The complex sweet-and-sour quality of this vinegar makes a perfect (one-ingredient) sauce, which is why so many restaurants use it.

pan-grilled pork chops on
corn and red pepper chutney

Corn makes a crunchy and sweet base for this spicy chop. Choose fresh, frozen, or canned corn; it's all good. We particularly like that Southwestern standby in a can, Mexican-style corn. Add a hit of chopped fresh red bell pepper if you have it.

1 tablespoon garlic powder

1 tablespoon paprika

1 tablespoon chili powder

½ teaspoon salt

Freshly milled black pepper

Pinch of cayenne

4 pork chops (1-inch-thick cut)

Cooking spray

2 tablespoons olive oil

1 small yellow onion, chopped

1 (16-ounce) can Mexican-style corn, rinsed and drained

1 red bell pepper, chopped

makes 4 servings
time: 15 minutes

1 Make the dry rub.
In a shallow bowl, use a fork to mix the garlic powder, paprika, chili powder, salt, and pepper to taste (more or less 1 teaspoon).

2 Prep the chops.
Thoroughly dry each chop, and rub them with the spice mixture. Use the remaining rub for the corn.

3 Cook the chops.
Heat a heavy medium skillet for 2 minutes. Spritz with cooking spray. Place the chops in the skillet and sauté until golden, about 5 minutes. Turn; then cook the other side for 5 more minutes, or until done. Remove from the skillet, and hold on a warm plate.

4 Sauté the corn and pepper.
Reduce the heat to medium, add the olive oil and onion to the same skillet, and cook for 3 minutes. Add the drained corn, red pepper, and remaining dry rub. Cook for 3 minutes. Top with the cooked chops, and serve from the skillet.

pan-grilled rosemary lamb chops on white beans with tomato

Want your kitchen to be awarded four stars? Take a moment to "French" those chops before you cook them. All that means is you stand each chop on end and run the blade of a chef's knife up against the bone to clean up the meaty part. Too much trouble? Just say "abracadabra" when you serve it forth. The aroma of lamb, rosemary, and olive oil will probably do the trick.

4 lamb loin chops (about 4 ounces each)

2 tablespoons olive oil

2 tablespoons fresh rosemary (2 teaspoons dried)

   Salt and freshly milled pepper

2 garlic cloves, chopped

1 (16-ounce) can cannellini or Great Northern beans, rinsed and drained

1 (12-ounce) can tomatoes

makes 4 servings
time: 20 minutes

1 Heat the skillet.

Heat a black skillet over high heat for 3 to 5 minutes, and then spray with a little cooking spray.

2 Pan-grill the chops.

Dry the chops thoroughly, and rub them with 1 tablespoon of the olive oil, 1 tablespoon of the rosemary, and salt and pepper to taste. Cook the chops over medium-high heat for 3 to 5 minutes per side, or to desired level of doneness. Remove the chops from the skillet, and keep them warm on a plate.

3 Cook the beans.

Lower the heat and add the remaining tablespoon of olive oil, rosemary, and garlic to the skillet. Cook for 1 minute. Stir in the beans, tomatoes, and salt and pepper to taste. Cook for 5 minutes. Top with the chops and serve from the skillet.

pan-grilled veal chops on green olive coulis

Canned green olives get top billing for martinis and relish trays but not much else. Capers in a jar, anchovy paste in a toothpaste tube, and canned olives all last forever and should always be in your bag of tricks.

4 (½-pound) veal loin chops (1 inch thick)
2 tablespoons olive oil
Salt and freshly milled pepper
Capers (for garnish)

**makes 4 servings
time: 20 minutes**

Green Olive Coulis

2 tablespoons olive oil, plus more for rubbing chops
1 medium onion, chopped
1 tablespoon anchovy paste (or 1 anchovy fillet, chopped)
¾ cup pitted green olives, chopped
2 tablespoons capers, slightly chopped
1 tablespoon fresh rosemary, finely chopped (1 teaspoon dried)
2 garlic cloves, chopped
Juice and zest of ½ lemon (2 tablespoons lemon juice; reserve some zest for garnish)
1½ cups white wine

1 Prepare the chops.

Dry the chops with a paper towel; then rub them with olive oil and salt and pepper to taste.

2 Make the coulis.

Heat a medium skillet on high heat for 2 minutes. Reduce the heat to medium, add the oil, and heat for 1 more minute. Add the onion, and cook for 5 minutes. Stir in the anchovy paste, green olives, capers, rosemary, and garlic, and cook for 2 minutes, stirring constantly.

3 Reduce the coulis.

Add the lemon juice and zest and the white wine to deglaze the pan, scraping up the browned bits from the bottom. Continue cooking on medium heat for 7 to 10 minutes, until the liquid is reduced by half.

4 Meanwhile, cook the chops.

Heat a large dry skillet for 3 to 4 minutes on high. Reduce the heat to medium-high, and pan-grill the chops for 4 to 6 minutes per side, until cooked to desired level of doneness.

5 Assemble the plates.

Spoon the olive coulis onto individual plates or a large platter, and top with the chops. Garnish the top of the chops with lemon zest strips and a few capers scattered on the plate.

pan-grilled veal chops on marinated mushrooms and garlic

Marinated mushrooms from a jar seasoned with their vinegary flavor and a little browned garlic make a wonderful mouthwatering base for veal. Say good-bye to rotting fresh mushrooms in the back of your refrigerator. Marinated mushrooms are pantry items. Cook the garlic right in the baking dish, and you minimize the number of dirty dishes, too.

¼ cup olive oil

2 garlic cloves, minced

3 (8-ounce) jars marinated mushrooms, drained and chopped

4 veal rib chops (1 to 1½ inch thick)

Salt and freshly milled pepper

¼ cup chopped fresh parsley (for garnish)

makes 4 servings
time: 25 minutes

1 Preheat the oven to 400° F.

2 Make the base.
At the bottom of a 13 × 9 × 2-inch glass or ceramic baking dish, stir together 2 tablespoons of the olive oil and the garlic. Microwave on HIGH (100 percent power) for 2 minutes. Stir in the mushrooms.

3 Prepare the chops.
Rub the chops with 1 tablespoon of the olive oil and salt and pepper to taste. Set aside while you heat the dry skillet.

4 Sear the chops.
Heat a large skillet on high heat for 2 minutes. Reduce the heat to medium-high, add the remaining olive oil, and sear the chops for 2 minutes per side. The chops will be golden brown on the outside and rare on the inside. (They will finish cooking in the oven.) Set aside on a plate.

5 Finish the dish.

Top the mushroom mixture with the seared chops. Place on the center rack of the preheated oven. Cook for 15 to 18 minutes, or to desired level of doneness. Internal temperature should be 135° to 140°F.

6 Assemble the dish.

Remove the chops from the oven. Arrange the mushrooms on a large platter with the chops on top. Sprinkle with the chopped parsley. Serve warm.

sautéed scallops in a citrus-curry sauce

Company coming? Want to wow 'em? You can do it easily if you have a can of coconut milk and some curry powder to jump-start a sauce. Sear scallops, then serve them in a pool of this liquid gold and watch your guests glow. The saffron-colored sauce is hot, sweet, sour, and bitter, all at once. Substitute frozen shrimp, try it with a chicken breast—this is a sauce to make any entrée sing. (We've even napped some sugar snap peas with the sauce.) A side of Chinese restaurant white rice, steamed broccoli with a squirt of clementine sauce—it's done.

12 diver scallops (or large shrimp peeled and deveined)

1 teaspoon chopped garlic

1 teaspoon sugar

Juice of 1 lime

Juice of 1 clementine, tangerine, or orange

½ teaspoon hot red pepper flakes

1 teaspoon chili oil

1 tablespoon fish sauce

1 tablespoon water

½ teaspoon rice vinegar

2 tablespoons peanut oil

makes 4 to 6 servings
time: 20 minutes or less

Curry Sauce

1 tablespoon Madras curry powder

1 (14-ounce) can coconut milk

2 tablespoons fish sauce

1 tablespoon sugar

½ cup minced cilantro

1 Marinate the scallops.

Toss the scallops with the garlic, sugar, lime and clementine juices, red pepper flakes and chili oil, fish sauce, water, and vinegar. Cover the scallops and set them aside for 10 to 15 minutes.

2 Make the curry sauce.

Dry fry the curry powder for a few moments in a small saucepan, just until it begins to become fragrant, then pour in the coconut milk, fish sauce, and sugar. Stir well and bring to a boil. Boil until the sauce is reduced by half.

3 Sauté the scallops.

Remove the scallops from the marinade and pat dry. Add the marinade to the curry sauce. Heat a large sauté pan with the peanut oil to the smoking point. Place the scallops in the skillet without overcrowding, making sure they lie on their flat surfaces. Sear for 3 to 4 minutes without moving them, then turn them once and cook for 2 to 3 minutes.

4 Finish the sauce.

Return the sauce to a boil while the scallops cook.

5 Serve.

Pool ¼ cup of sauce in each warmed dinner plate and arrange 3 scallops in the center of the plate. Sprinkle with fresh cilantro.

spaghetti-sauce sorcery

Marinara has become a staple for the half-scratch cook, but even the most enthusiastic noodlers get tired of pasta with red sauce week in, week out. Living with this quandary on a weekly basis motivated us to come up with more than ten alternative uses for this joy in a jar. Using marinara saves on the simmer time—after all, they did the simmering at the marinara factory. You just have to add a few other ingredients and voilà, you have some interesting stews, most of them miles away from anything you'd associate with a red-checked tablecloth.

1. **Mediterranean Seafood Stew**

2. **Fast Shrimp Gumbo**

3. **Middle-Eastern Sausage Stew**

4. **Vietnamese Chicken Stew**

5. **Tortilla, Corn, and Chicken Stew**

6. **Smoky Mustard-Greens Soup**

7. **Shirley Barr's Twenty-Minute Meat Loaf**

8. **Chicken, Tomato, and Leek Stew**

9. **Absolutely Easy Pasta with Vodka Sauce**

10. **Sicilian Pasta with Tuna**

11. **Fettuccine with Creamy Marinara and Italian Sweet Sausage**

mediterranean seafood stew

Who knew instant rice would make a comeback? But cooked in high-end chicken broth, it is really great. This is a meal in a pot that is full of rich flavors and on the table in less than half an hour. What could be bad?

3 cups chicken broth (we prefer the organic variety in a carton)

1 (3½-ounce) bag instant rice

2 tablespoons olive oil

3 fish fillets*

1 (25-ounce) jar marinara, preferably with roasted red pepper (or flavor of your choice)

1 cup frozen peas

1 bay leaf

1 teaspoon Tabasco

Salt and freshly milled pepper

makes 4 servings
time: 20 minutes

1 Cook the rice.

In a large pot, bring the chicken broth and rice to a boil. Cover, and cook for 5 minutes.

2 Brown the fish.

Film the bottom of a medium skillet with olive oil, and heat the oil on medium-high heat for 1 minute. Thoroughly dry the fish, and sauté it for 3 minutes on each side. The fish will be firmed up and just beginning to brown. Remove to a cutting board, and cut into chunks, discarding any bones.

3 Make the stew.

Add the marinara, frozen peas, bay leaf, and fish chunks to the rice and chicken broth, bring to a boil, then reduce the heat and simmer for 5 minutes.

4 Season the stew.

Add the Tabasco and salt and pepper to taste, remove the bay leaf, and serve.

* Any firm-fleshed white fish such as sea bass, cod, or orange roughy works here. We love the frozen orange roughy fillets from Costco. If using frozen fish, flash-thaw it in a bowl of warm water before sautéing.

fast shrimp gumbo

Being originally from Houston, we have eaten our share of gumbos. In fact, we've been to gumbo cook-offs in the parking lots of local high schools, the Astrodome— you name it. In other words, we know gumbo, and to our tastes this fast version is quite acceptable. Gumbo base traditionally is cooked for hours; by starting with a jar of marinara, you let the manufacturers do the simmering, and you get all the raves.

makes 4 servings
time: 30 minutes

2 tablespoons olive oil

1 carrot, chopped

1 stalk celery, chopped

1 large onion, chopped

1 tablespoon all-purpose flour

3 cups chicken broth (we prefer the organic variety in a box)

1 (3½-ounce) bag instant rice

1 (8-ounce) bottle clam juice

1 (25-ounce) jar basic marinara

1 cup frozen sliced okra

1 bay leaf

1 teaspoon thyme

1 teaspoon Tabasco sauce

Salt and freshly milled pepper

1 pound frozen peeled and deveined shrimp or frozen shellfish mix

1 Make the roux.

Coat the bottom of a large Dutch oven or heavy soup pot with the olive oil. Heat the oil over medium-high heat for 1 minute. Stir in the carrots, celery, and onion, and sauté for 5 minutes. Add the flour, and sauté for 3 to 5 more minutes, or until the flour just becomes golden brown.

2 Flavor the rice.

Add the chicken broth and rice, bring to a boil, and cook for 5 minutes. Add the clam juice, marinara, okra, bay leaf, and thyme. Bring to a boil, and cook for 5 minutes longer.

3 Finish the gumbo.

Add the Tabasco, salt and pepper to taste, and the shrimp, and cook for 5 to 10 minutes, until the shrimp just turns pink. Serve at once.

middle-eastern sausage stew

The enticing flavors of Middle-Eastern cuisine held sway over European tables from the eleventh century until the Moors' four-hundred-year occupation. This stew is spicy, savory, and best of all, you can have it on the table faster than you can say Ali Baba.

serves 4
time: 25 minutes

2 tablespoons olive oil

1 carrot, chopped

1 stalk celery, chopped

1 large onion, chopped

1 pound veal, chicken, or turkey sausage (Bruce Aidells Apple & Chicken or even sweet Italian is good)

1 bay leaf

$\frac{1}{2}$ teaspoon ground cinnamon

$\frac{1}{2}$ teaspoon ground ginger

1 teaspoon freshly milled pepper

3 cups chicken broth (we prefer the organic variety in a box)

1 ($3\frac{1}{2}$-ounce) bag instant rice

1 (25-ounce) jar basic marinara sauce

Salt

1 Sauté the base.

Coat the bottom of a large Dutch oven or pot with olive oil. Heat the oil on medium-high heat for 1 minute. Stir in the carrot, celery, onion, sausage, bay leaf, cinnamon, ginger, and pepper, and sauté for 5 to 7 minutes, stirring intermittently as needed.

2 Cook the rice.

Add the chicken broth and rice to the pot, and bring to a boil. Cook for 5 minutes.

3 Finish the stew.

Add the marinara, and taste to see if additional salt is needed. You may also want to add more chicken broth if you prefer a soupier consistency. Simmer for 10 minutes.

vietnamese chicken stew

This wonderful chicken stew is an adaptation of a dish served at one of NYC's most wonderful hole-in-the-wall Vietnamese restaurants. Using instant rice saves a whole cooking step, which is key when you don't have a minute to spare.

2 tablespoons vegetable oil

1 large onion, chopped

1 pound chicken breast fillets, split, pounded to $\frac{1}{2}$-inch thickness, and cut into bite-size pieces

3 garlic cloves, chopped

1 tablespoon chopped fresh ginger

1 teaspoon hot red pepper flakes

1 teaspoon sugar

1 teaspoon Vietnamese fish sauce (nuoc mam)

1 teaspoon freshly milled pepper

3 cups chicken broth (we prefer the organic variety in a box)

1 ($3\frac{1}{2}$-ounce) bag instant rice

2 cups sliced bok choy

1 (25-ounce) jar basic marinara sauce

Salt

makes 4 servings
time: 25 minutes

1 Cook the chicken.

Coat the bottom of a large Dutch oven or pot with the oil. Heat the oil on medium-high heat for 1 minute. Stir in the onion and chicken, and sauté for 10 minutes, stirring intermittently as needed, until the meat is opaque. Add the garlic, ginger, red pepper flakes, sugar, and fish sauce.

2 Cook the rice.

Add the pepper, chicken broth, rice, and bok choy, and bring to a boil. Cover and cook over medium heat for 5 minutes.

3 Finish the stew.

Add the marinara, and taste to see if additional salt is needed. You may also want to add more chicken broth if you like a soupier consistency. Simmer on medium heat for 10 minutes, and serve.

tortilla, corn, and chicken
stew

This version of chicken soup will cure anything that ails you. The marinara makes it rich in minutes.

2 tablespoons vegetable oil

1 large onion, chopped

1 stalk celery, chopped

1 pound chicken breast fillets, pounded to ½-inch thickness and cut into bite-size pieces

3 garlic cloves, chopped

½ (7-ounce) can chopped green chiles (use the whole can if you are feeling brave)

1 jalapeño pepper or smoked chipotle pepper, seeded and chopped

4 cups chicken broth (we prefer the organic variety in a box)

1 (25-ounce) jar basic marinara sauce

2 cups frozen corn

Salt and freshly milled pepper

4 corn tortillas, sliced into thin strips

Sour cream (for garnish)

makes 4 servings
time: 25 minutes

1 Cook the chicken.

Coat the bottom of a large Dutch oven or pot with the oil, and heat the oil on medium-high heat for 1 minute. Stir in the onion, celery, and chicken, and sauté until the chicken is opaque, about 10 minutes, stirring intermittently as needed. Add the garlic, green chiles, and jalapeño pepper, and cook for 1 more minute.

2 Deglaze the pan.

Add the chicken broth and stir, scraping up the brown bits from the bottom of the pan.

3 Finish the stew.

Add the marinara, corn, and some additional chicken stock if you prefer a soupier stew. Taste to see if additional salt and pepper are needed. Lower the heat to medium, and simmer for 5 minutes.

4 Add the tortillas.

Just before you serve the stew, stir in the tortilla strips, and cook for 5 minutes more. Garnish with a dollop of sour cream, and serve at once.

smoky mustard-greens soup

Okay—so this recipe is huge. You'll be glad. You can eat it for several nights running, or freeze part of it for one of those nights when you can't even face the idea of cooking dinner. Substitute fresh or frozen spinach if you wish.

12 ounces Italian sweet sausage, removed from casings

3 slices bacon, chopped

1 cup chopped yellow onion

2 garlic cloves, smashed

1 (16-ounce) can chicken broth

2 cups basic marinara sauce

Salt and freshly milled pepper

6 cups fresh or frozen mustard greens, ribs removed, greens chopped

makes 8 servings
time: less than 30 minutes

1 Sauté the meat and aromatics.

Heat a large soup pot over medium-high heat. Add the sausage and bacon, and cook until they brown, about 10 minutes. Add the onion and garlic about halfway through, and stir until softened. Drain excess fat.

2 Make the soup.

Deglaze the pan with the broth; then stir in the marinara and salt and pepper to taste. Cook over medium heat for 10 minutes. Add the mustard greens, and simmer the soup just long enough to wilt the greens, no more than 3 to 5 minutes. They should still be bright green and tender.

3 Serve.

Ladle the soup into rimmed soup bowls. May be made ahead, refrigerated, and gently reheated.

shirley barr's twenty-minute meat loaf

Sure, we all love meat loaf, but it takes too much time and too much work to get it oven ready, right? Wrong. Do as our friend Shirley does. Use a jar of marinara sauce and your food processor, and you can have it ready in five minutes. Press it flat like a pizza, and it cooks in twenty minutes. You'll be in and out of the kitchen in a flash. What's not to like?

1 medium onion, halved

2 garlic cloves

½ cup fresh parsley

⅔ cup Italian-seasoned bread crumbs

1 teaspoon oregano

1 large egg

1 pound (85-percent-lean) ground beef (or turkey)

Salt and freshly milled pepper

1 cup basic marinara sauce

½ cup grated mozzarella cheese

3 tablespoons grated Parmesan cheese

1 cup pizza-style toppings of your choice: thinly sliced mushrooms, onions, bell peppers, and the like

makes 4 servings
time: 30 minutes

1 Prepare the pan.

Preheat the oven to 350°F. Spritz a 9-inch square baking pan with cooking spray.

2 Assemble the dish.

Place the onion, garlic, and parsley in the food processor, and pulse to chop coarsely. Add the bread crumbs, oregano, and egg, and pulse to combine. Add ground meat and salt and pepper to taste, and pulse to mix. Pat into the prepared baking pan. Pour marinara sauce over; top with cheeses and vegetables.

3 Bake and serve.

Bake for 20 minutes. Cut into squares, and serve hot.

chicken, tomato, and
leek stew

Chicken wings make a splendid soup base. Flavorful, fast to cook, and easy. Serve over the leftover Chinese rice you probably have lurking in the back of the fridge.

2	tablespoons butter	
2	slices bacon, chopped	
1	pound chicken wings	
2	medium leeks, thoroughly washed and cut into 1-inch pieces, including 2 inches of green	
1	tablespoon tarragon	
1	cup basic marinara sauce	
½	cup heavy cream	
	Salt and freshly milled pepper	
4	cups cooked rice	

makes 6 servings
time: 30 minutes

1 Make the stew base.

In a large soup pot, melt the butter, and add the bacon. Cook for 3 to 5 minutes over medium heat, until the bacon is limp. Stir in the chicken, and cook for 2 minutes. Add the leeks, tarragon, and marinara. Cook for about 15 minutes, or until the chicken is golden and the leeks are tender.

2 Finish the soup.

Add 1 quart of water, scraping up the browned bits from the bottom of the pot to deglaze the pan. Reduce the heat to medium, and cook until the chicken is tender, about 10 more minutes. Stir in the cream, and simmer for a few minutes. Adjust the seasonings with salt and pepper. If you wish, fish out the chicken wings, remove the meat, and add it back to the soup. Discard the skin and bones. Better yet, let the diners at the table do this. The flavor is lovely.

3 Serve.

Pour the stew over cooked rice, and serve hot.

absolutely easy pasta with
vodka sauce

It is a fact that you are no better than your pantry. And the success of your magical dinners may very well rest with the quality of the ingredients you keep on hand. Make this Roman dish with cheap vodka, second-rate marinara, or milk instead of cream, and you will not be happy. Use the best ingredients you can. It's worth it.

As for the pasta, there are choices. Our neighborhood trattoria, which inspired this recipe, layers stuffed rigatoni with this pink sauce. At home, we often simply use best quality dried egg fettuccine. Use what you have, give yourself twenty minutes, and you'll have a satisfying dinner.

2 tablespoons salt	
4½ ounces dried egg fettuccine or filled pasta of your choice	makes 2 servings
3 tablespoons butter	time: 20 minutes
⅛ teaspoon hot red pepper flakes	
½ cup Absolut (or other best quality) vodka	
1 cup basic marinara sauce	
½ cup heavy cream	
Salt and freshly milled pepper	
½ cup freshly grated Parmesan	

1 Cook the pasta.

Bring 4 quarts of water to boil over high heat. Add the salt, and then throw in the pasta and cook according to package directions.

2 Make the sauce.

In a skillet large enough to hold the pasta as well as the sauce, melt the butter over medium heat. Add the red pepper flakes, and cook for about 30 seconds. Add the vodka, and boil for 2 minutes. Stir in the marinara sauce and cream, season to taste with salt and pepper, and simmer for about 5 minutes.

3 Serve.

Once the pasta is cooked, drain well and then add it to the sauce along with the cheese. Toss to mix thoroughly, then divide between 2 dinner plates. Serve at once.

sicilian pasta with tuna

You may have to look a bit to find Italian-style tuna packed in oil, but the taste is so superior, you'll never return to that awful, dry, flaky-as-peeling-plaster stuff they pass off as tuna packed in "spring water." You want tuna? Get the good stuff.

¾ pound linguine

1 (26-ounce) jar green and black olive pasta sauce

1 (6-ounce) can imported Italian solid white albacore tuna in oil, drained and flaked

Kalamata olives, pitted (for garnish)

makes 4 servings
time: 20 minutes

1 Cook the pasta.

Bring a large pot of water to a boil, add salt, and then cook the linguine, following package directions. Reserve ½ cup of the pasta water. Drain the pasta, and return it to the pot with the reserved pasta water.

2 Heat pasta sauce.

Meanwhile, heat the sauce in a medium saucepan to just under a boil. Add the tuna, and heat through for about 2 minutes.

3 Serve.

Divide the pasta among 4 rimmed soup or pasta bowls. Top with the sauce, and serve at once, garnishing with additional kalamata olives.

fettuccine with creamy marinara and italian sweet sausage

Got a jar of marinara and some cream? You're more than halfway to a sophisti-cated supper in almost no time and with almost no effort. No sausage? Guess it's your night to be a vegetarian.

¾ pound fettuccine or other pasta

1 tablespoon extra-virgin olive oil

2 shallots or 1 small onion, minced

2 garlic cloves, minced

1 pound Italian sweet sausage, casings removed (optional)

1 (28-ounce) jar basic marinara sauce

1 cup heavy cream

1 cup frozen peas (optional)

Parmesan cheese

Hot red pepper flakes

makes 4 servings
time: 15 minutes or less

1 Cook the pasta.

Bring 4 quarts of water to a boil in a large pot. Salt generously; then add the fettuccine, and cook according to the package directions until al dente, about 5 minutes.

2 Make the sauce.

Heat the oil in a large skillet, then sauté the shallots and garlic until translucent, about 5 minutes. Add the sausage, if using, and cook through, about 5 minutes longer. Stir in the marinara sauce and cream, and bring to just below a boil. Cook for 5 minutes. Just before serving, stir in the optional peas. Cover and let the sauce stand for about 3 minutes to heat the peas.

3 Serve.

Drain the pasta, and divide it among 4 warmed dinner plates. Spoon the sauce into a lake in the middle of the pasta. Serve at once, with the Parmesan and red pepper flakes at the table.

condiment genie

Kitchen alchemy begins in the condiment jar. As far back as the fourteenth century B.C., jars of mixed herbs and spices were found in Tutankhamen's tomb, buried with the king so that he might have his favorite dishes on the other side. This makes perfect sense to us, since we can't imagine any celestial kitchen without these heavenly flavor makers. They're that indispensable.

It's amazing what tricks you can pull off with a jar of mayo or mustard, and that's just the beginning. You can now buy excellent chutneys, pestos, caponata, and more, any one of which provides that sleight-of-hand flavor boost that will make you look like a hero every time.

We've recommended some of our hands-down winners and told you what to do with them in this section. The variety is endless, but the quality variations are extreme, so if we say to buy Best Foods or Hellman's mayonnaise, we mean it. Generic mayos we banish without a backward glance.

The same is true for salad dressings. At least 90 percent of the bottled glop should be poured out into the desert. But exceptions make the rule, and we call your attention to Annie's, found at fine supermarkets.

When it comes to mustard, give us good old Dijon anytime. You can cook with it. You can thicken a sauce with it. Dijon is a must on every pantry shelf.

Our barbecue-sauce focus group (that would be Katherine, Gordon, Linda, Lily, and Noel—the last two aged four and way picky about barbecue sauces) votes unanimously for K.C. Masterpiece. Yes, the very same one you can buy in the giant plastic squeeze bottle at warehouse clubs.

1. Curry Mayonnaise

2. Lime–Mango Chutney Mayonnaise

3. Mayonnaise with Garlic and Thyme

4. Scotch Sauce

5. **Mustard with Capers**

6. **Sour Cream and Mustard with Scallions**

7. **Sherrill's Jarlsberg Swiss Artichoke Spread**

8. **Cheese-Stuffed Chiles**

9. **Tropical Fruit and Shrimp Salad**

10. **Back at the Ranch Layered Salad**

11. **Curried Crab and Water-Chestnut Filled Endive**

12. **French Chicken Wings**

13. **North-African Chicken Wings**

14. **North-African Chicken Wing Dip**

15. **Easy Buffalo Wings**

16. **Porterhouse Steaks with Bourbon, Bacon, and Barbecue Sauce**

17. **Teriyaki Tuna with Blueberry Chutney**

18. **Grilled Lamb Chops on Caponata**

19. **Grilled Lamb Chops on Sweet-and-Sour Red-Pepper Chutney**

curry mayonnaise

Curry is the original magical dinner spice. It adds color and life to anything it is mixed with.

2 teaspoons curry powder

½ cup mayonnaise

½ cup sour cream

Salt and freshly milled pepper

makes 1 cup
time: 5 minutes

1 Toast the curry powder.

In the toaster oven in a small, dry skillet, heat the curry powder for 30 seconds on medium heat, watching closely so that you don't burn it.

2 Make the sauce.

Stir the mayonnaise, sour cream, and curry powder together. Season to taste with the salt and pepper.

lime–mango chutney
mayonnaise

Mango chutney, mayonnaise, and limes—all cabinet staples. Mixed together, these ingredients make for a wonderfully complex sauce that's good for almost anything.

1 **cup mayonnaise**

½ **cup mango chutney**

Juice of 1 lime

makes 1 cup
time: 5 minutes

Make the mayonnaise.

Stir the mayonnaise, chutney, and lime juice together until well blended.

mayonnaise with garlic and thyme

Garlic, thyme, mayonnaise—millions of French people can't be wrong.

1 cup mayonnaise

2 garlic cloves, minced or pressed

1 teaspoon thyme

Juice of 1 lemon

makes 1 cup
time: 5 minutes

Make the mayonnaise.
Stir the mayonnaise, garlic, thyme, and lemon juice together until smooth.

scotch sauce

This Belgian sauce is wonderful on red meat or greens. Take a shot of scotch for yourself.

1 cup mayonnaise

2 tablespoons ketchup

2 tablespoons scotch

¼ teaspoon cayenne (or less)

makes 1 cup
time: 5 minutes

Make the sauce.

Stir the mayonnaise, ketchup, scotch, and pepper together.

mustard with capers

The sour tang of the capers and the spicy mustard complement each other well.

1 cup mustard

¼ cup plus 2 tablespoons capers, drained and slightly mashed

makes 1 cup
time: 5 minutes

Make the mustard.

Stir the mustard and capers together.

sour cream and mustard
with scallions

Here's a sauce for your favorite grilled meat, be it pork, beef, or veal.

4 or 5 scallions, thinly sliced

1 cup sour cream

2 teaspoons Dijon mustard

2 teaspoons lemon juice

Salt and freshly milled pepper

makes 1 cup
time: 5 minutes

Make the sauce.

Stir the scallions, sour cream, mustard, lemon juice, and salt and pepper to taste together.

sherrill's jarlsberg swiss artichoke spread

Here's a recipe that has circulated since the 1960s, back when processed foods were processed foods. It is worth reviving. If you can lay hands on a cup of fresh crabmeat, throw that in—too good.

1 (6- to 8-ounce) jar artichokes, drained

2 garlic cloves

1 cup coarsely diced Jarlsberg Swiss cheese

1 cup best-quality mayonnaise

Salt, pepper, and paprika

makes 8 to 10 servings
time: 30 minutes

1 Prepare the filling.

Preheat the oven to 350°F. Add the artichokes to a food processor, along with the garlic, cheese, and mayonnaise. Process to make a rough purée. Taste, and season with the salt, pepper, and paprika.

2 Bake and serve.

Transfer the spread to a small casserole, and bake for 25 minutes. Serve warm with crackers or crudités.

cheese-stuffed chiles

Crank open that can. Pull out the goat cheese and Jack. You're on your way to one charmed starter. Bubble, toil, and no trouble. You'll like it.

8 whole fire-roasted chiles
(8-ounce can)

½ pound fresh goat cheese

½ pound Monterey Jack cheese, cut into 8 (3 × ½-inch) straws

1 cup fresh or prepared salsa

Tortilla chips

makes 8 appetizer servings
time: 15 minutes or less

1 Prepare chiles.

Heat the oven to 400°F. Spritz an 8 × 8-inch baking dish with olive oil cooking spray. Using your fingers, gently open the chiles at the top, taking care not to tear them. Remove and discard the seeds and membranes. Divide the goat cheese into 8 pieces, and roll it into balls.

2 Stuff the chiles.

Insert a Jack cheese straw into each chile. Roll the goat cheese balls into slender torpedoes, and slide them into the openings on top of the Jack cheese. Arrange the chiles in the baking dish, and top with the salsa. Bake until bubbly and hot, about 10 minutes.

3 Serve.

Remove the chiles from the oven; let them stand for a few moments, then cut each chile into 1-inch pieces. Arrange them on tortilla chips on a decorative platter, and pass them around.

tropical fruit and shrimp salad

Sweet little bay shrimp are so good when you can find them not prefrozen. If you have to use the frozen, thawed ones, toss them with ½ teaspoon honey to begin to bring back the sweetness.

1 pound fresh cooked bay shrimp

½ cup red onion cut into thin rings

1 cup raspberry vinaigrette

1 (10-ounce) package bitter salad greens

1 ripe mango, peeled and cut into small chunks

2 kiwi, peeled and sliced into rings

1 cup raspberries or strawberries

1 tablespoon black sesame seeds

makes 4 servings
time: 10 minutes

1 Prepare the salad.
Toss the shrimp and onion with ½ cup of the vinaigrette. Cover and refrigerate for 20 minutes to marinate. Drain, and discard the dressing.

2 Serve.
To arrange the salads, divide the salad greens among 4 cold plates. Divide the shrimp mixture among the plates. Top with mango, kiwi, and raspberries. Sprinkle black sesame seeds over all. Serve the remaining dressing on the side.

back at the ranch layered salad

This good-looking salad has been a showstopper since the 1960s, when people first began layering salads. So much easier now, with pretorn lettuces and pre-cooked bacon. At the deli in our grocery store, they even sell boiled eggs. Who needs the cook?

1 (10-ounce) package or 8 cups torn romaine lettuce leaves

1 pint grape tomatoes

1 medium hothouse cucumber, chopped

4 hard-cooked eggs, chopped

1 (10-ounce) package cooked bacon, crumbled

1 small red onion, chopped

1 cup buttermilk ranch dressing

makes 4 servings
time: 20 minutes
plus chilling time

1 Compose the salad.

Choose a clear glass salad bowl, and arrange the lettuce leaves on the bottom. Pulse the tomatoes in the food processor to make a rough chop; then layer them over the lettuce. Add the cucumber, chopped eggs, bacon, and onion. Spread the dressing evenly over the top. Cover with plastic wrap, and chill for at least 30 minutes and up to 24 hours.

2 Serve.

Toss the salad, and invite people to dig in.

curried crab and water-chestnut filled endive

The sweet flavor of ready-to-go crabmeat, available at most better grocery stores, is an excellent contrast to the spicy curry and the bitter endive. Water chestnuts add a nice crunch.

6 ounces cooked crabmeat, picked over for shells*	makes 4 servings
¼ cup mayonnaise	time: 30 minutes
2 tablespoons chopped water chestnuts	
1 teaspoon curry powder (we love Madras or Sunrise)	
Freshly milled pepper	
3 to 4 medium heads Belgian endive, leaves separated from each other	

1 Make the filling.

In a bowl, mix the crab, mayonnaise, water chestnuts, curry powder, and black pepper to taste. Blend gently.

2 Stuff the endive.

Spoon 1 heaping teaspoon of the crab mixture onto the bottom of the endive leaves.

3 Compose the plate.

Arrange the filled endive leaves in concentric circles on the plate, and refrigerate until serving time.

*Do not even consider artificial crab.

french chicken wings

If you would dare to call French dressing French, then you can surely call these wings the same. Actually, we just know that mixing common French dressing with common dried French onion soup mix makes a great flavoring for chicken wings, a distinctly American invention. Or rather we should explain a marketing scheme that worked wonderfully. Five years ago, they couldn't give the damn wings away; now people are flocking to the store for them. Much to our chagrin, we've discovered wings are our favorite, especially when stirred together with these two cliché American condiments.

1	cup French dressing
½	cup dark corn syrup
1	(1.4-ounce) package French onion soup mix
1	tablespoon Worcestershire sauce
2 to 3	pounds chicken wings

makes 24 appetizers
or 6 dinner servings
time: 30 minutes

1 Make the sauce.

Mix the dressing, corn syrup, soup mix, and Worcestershire sauce together in a 13 × 9 × 2-inch pan. Add the chicken wings, and toss them to coat on all sides.

2 Cook the wings.

Heat the oven to 500°F. Bake the wings for 20 minutes, turn the wings, and bake for an additional 5 minutes. Serve them hot or at room temperature.

north-african chicken wings

India meets the dark continent smothered by a French Colonial layer of mayonnaise.

2 pounds chicken wings

1 cup best-quality mayonnaise

1 cup bread crumbs

1 teaspoon chili powder

1 teaspoon garam masala

½ teaspoon cayenne

½ teaspoon salt

makes 12 appetizers
or 4 servings
time: 30 minutes

1 Prepare the wings.

Preheat the oven to 500°F. Spritz a 13 × 9 × 2-inch baking dish with cooking spray. Slather wings with mayonnaise in a bowl.

2 Make the coating.

In a pie pan, mix the crumbs with all the seasonings. Dredge the chicken wings in this mix, and lay them in a single layer in the baking dish. Bake for 20 minutes, then turn, and bake for 5 minutes more. Serve hot or at room temperature.

north-african chicken
wing dip

If you want to tune up chicken wings you picked up at the deli, stir together this dip.

1/3 cup chunky peanut butter

1/2 cup coconut milk (or cream)

2 garlic cloves

1/4 cup water

1/4 cup chopped red or yellow bell pepper

1/8 teaspoon hot red pepper flakes

1 teaspoon soy sauce

Cilantro leaves (for garnish)

makes 1 cup
time: 10 minutes

Make the sauce.

In the bowl of a food processor fitted with the steel blade, mix all the ingredients except the cilantro. Process until smooth, about 1 minute. Transfer the dip to a serving bowl, and top with the cilantro leaves. Serve at once with chicken wings.

easy buffalo wings

Forget all those complicated methods for deep-frying chicken wings. Throw them in a pan, lob them into a scorching hot oven, and then finish with the traditional hot sauce and butter, a jar of commercial blue cheese or ranch dressing, and celery sticks. It's that easy.

1 cup mayonnaise	makes 6 servings
2 tablespoons Tabasco sauce	time: 30 minutes
3 pounds chicken wings	
¼ cup melted butter	
Blue cheese or ranch dressing	
Celery sticks	

1 Make the sauce.

In a mixing cup, combine the mayonnaise and Tabasco until smooth.

2 Cook the wings.

Preheat the oven to 500°F. Arrange the chicken wings one layer deep on baking sheets. Use a brush to slather the wings on all sides with the mayo. Bake until golden brown, about 25 minutes; then turn and finish cooking on the second side, about 5 minutes.

3 Serve.

Remove the wings to a serving platter, and drizzle them with the butter. Give a few shakes of the Tabasco bottle again. Pass the wings along with celery ribs and dip them in blue cheese or ranch dressing as you eat.

porterhouse steaks with bourbon, bacon, and barbecue sauce

Texans have long known the advantages of the four Bs—barbecue sauce, bourbon, bacon, and beef. By combining the use of the microwave and a skillet you don't even need a long Southern evening to get this meal on the table.

2 tablespoons olive oil

1 medium yellow onion, thinly sliced

4 slices bacon, chopped into 1/2-inch pieces

3/4 cup barbecue sauce

2 tablespoons bourbon

Salt and freshly milled pepper

2 large porterhouse steaks, also known as T-bones, the same thickness

2 tablespoons vegetable oil, plus more for rubbing steaks

1/4 cup chopped yellow onion (for garnish)

makes 4 servings
time: 25 minutes

1 Preheat the oven to 400° F.

2 Make the sauce.
In a 13 × 9 × 2-inch baking dish, stir together the olive oil, onion, and bacon. Microwave on HIGH (100 percent power) for 3 minutes. Stir, and cook for 3 more minutes. Stir in the barbecue sauce, bourbon, and the salt and pepper to taste; return to the microwave, and cook on HIGH for 3 more minutes.

3 Prepare the steaks.
Rub the steaks with vegetable oil, and salt and pepper.

4 Sear the steaks.
Heat a dry medium skillet on high for 2 minutes. Reduce the heat to medium-high, add the oil, and sear the steaks one at a time for 1 to 2 minutes per side. Toss the steaks in the barbecue sauce, and place the baking dish on the center rack of the oven. Cook for 10 minutes, or until desired level of doneness. Internal temperature should be 135° to 140°F. for rare.

5 Serve.
Remove the dish from the oven. Spoon the barbecue sauce mixture onto individual plates. Top with a piece of meat. Garnish with chopped onions. Serve warm.

teriyaki tuna with blueberry chutney

No-kitchen cooking in summer calls for outdoor grills combined with simple stir-together condiments. We adore fresh blueberries in season dumped into a bowl and whizzed up into a quick chutney that makes a fine bed for grilled fish. Can't find fresh tuna? Substitute shark or salmon. Chutney keeps in the refrigerator for up to a week and also makes a fine accompaniment to roast chicken.

2 tablespoons teriyaki sauce

$\frac{1}{2}$ teaspoon cayenne

4 (6-ounce) tuna steaks

makes 4 servings
time: 20 minutes

Blueberry Chutney

1 pint fresh blueberries, washed and drained

$\frac{1}{2}$ cup finely chopped cucumber

1 small scallion, minced

Grated zest and 1 teaspoon juice of $\frac{1}{2}$ lemon

$\frac{1}{4}$ teaspoon fresh thyme leaves

$\frac{1}{2}$ teaspoon salt

$\frac{1}{2}$ teaspoon freshly milled pepper

1 Prepare the fish.

Mix the teriyaki and cayenne in a resealable plastic bag. Add the tuna. Seal and refrigerate for 30 minutes or so while you heat the grill and stir together the chutney. Turn the tuna once or twice if you think of it.

2 Make the chutney.

In a medium bowl, combine the berries with all the remaining ingredients. Cover and set aside.

3 Grill fish.

Heat the grill, then lay the fish down about 4 inches from a hot fire and cook for 3 to 5 minutes per side, or until cooked to the desired doneness. Brush with more teriyaki marinade as it cooks.

4 Serve.

Mound the chutney on 4 plates, and top each with a grilled fish portion.

grilled lamb chops on
caponata

Glistening caponata, a mixture of eggplant, tomatoes, and olives, has been around for decades. Buy a couple of jars, and use it as a base for chops. This recipe uses a chef's trick of searing meat in a skillet and finishing it in the oven. That way the juices are locked in, the caponata is warmed to perfection, and you didn't even break a sweat.

8 lamb loin chops (1 inch thick)

2 tablespoons olive oil, plus more for the baking dish and skillet

Salt and freshly milled pepper

3 (7-ounce) jars caponata

Lemon zest and a few capers (for garnish)

makes 4 servings
time: 25 minutes

1 Preheat the oven to 400° F.

2 Sear the chops.
Rub the chops with the olive oil, and salt and pepper to taste. Heat a dry medium skillet on high for 2 minutes. Reduce the heat to medium-high, coat with olive oil, and sear the chops for 2 minutes per side in 2 batches of 4, so as not to crowd the pan. The chops will be golden brown on the outside and rare on the inside. They will finish cooking in the oven. Keep them warm on a plate.

3 Finish the dish.
Grease a 13 × 9 × 2-inch baking dish with olive oil. Spread the caponata at the bottom of dish, and arrange the seared chops on top. Place the dish on the center rack of the oven, and cook for 15 minutes or to desired level of doneness. Internal temperature should be 135°F for medium rare.

4 Serve.
Arrange the chops on a large platter with the caponata beneath, and top with lemon zest and a few capers. Serve warm.

grilled lamb chops on sweet-and-sour red-pepper chutney

The gamey flavor of lamb stands up very well to the bright sweet-and-sour flavor of this fifteen-minute microwavable chutney. We buy jars of roasted red peppers by the dozen because they are so versatile.

Sweet-and-Sour Red-Pepper Chutney

makes 4 servings
time: 25 minutes

- 1 onion, quartered
- ¼ cup olive oil, plus more for rubbing chops
- ½ cup balsamic vinegar
- ¼ cup sugar
- ¾ teaspoon salt
- 1 teaspoon mustard seed
- ¼ to ½ teaspoon hot red pepper flakes
- 2 (12-ounce) jars roasted red peppers

Lamb Chops

- 8 lamb rib chops (about 2 ounces each)—Frenched, if you wish*
- 1 tablespoon olive oil
- Salt and freshly milled pepper
- Sprigs of mint (for garnish)

1 Cook the onions.

Place the onion quarters in the bowl of a food processor, and give them 4 pulses to chop coarsely. Remove the blade, stir in the olive oil, and place the bowl in the microwave. Cook on HIGH (100 percent power) for 6 minutes, stirring once at the 3-minute mark to soften and caramelize the sugar in the onion.

2 Finish the sauce.

Return the bowl of the food processor to the base, and replace the blade. Add the vinegar, sugar, salt, mustard seed, red pepper flakes, and drained roasted red peppers, and pulse 3 times to combine the ingredients. Remove the blade, return the sauce to the microwave, and cook for 6 minutes.

3 Meanwhile, heat the grill.

Heat the grill on high for 3 to 5 minutes.

4 Grill the chops.

Dry the meat thoroughly, and rub with olive oil and salt and pepper to taste. Grill the chops on medium-high heat for 3 to 5 minutes per side or to desired level of doneness.

5 Serve.

Serve by placing the chops on top of a bed of the chutney, leaning against each other with the bone standing up in the air. Garnish with a sprig of mint.

* Ask the butcher to French the chops. This simply means to cut away the cartilage and fat from the bone, leaving a nice clean smooth bone. If you are ambitious and have 10 minutes to dedicate to the project, you can do it yourself. Stand the chop up and rake a sharp knife against the bone, stripping away the meat two inches from the end; leave meat attached at the fleshy end of the chop. Turn and repeat until the bone is cleaned up.

chapter five *
the soup cauldron

Who hasn't used a can of chicken broth to make an impromptu soup? You know what we're talking about: You open a can of chicken broth. You root around in the back of the refrigerator for a Chinese takeout box of rice. You toss in three or four mushrooms. You whack a scallion into bits and add that. Finally, you whisk in some frozen peas and a raw egg. It's lunch in five minutes. That's old-fashioned white magic, the kind of card trick every graduate student learned trying to eat on the fly.

America's never-ending craving for quick, hot, satisfying meals has driven us to the soup kitchen for most of our lives. And while we have no quarrel with the Campbell's folks, we have come to adore a new generation of soups that are boxed, not canned, and have the huge advantage of being flavorful without being overly salty or sugared.

The brand we especially draw your attention to is Imagine Natural. These shelf-stable, asceptically packaged boxed soups from California are excellent. We can buy them at Whole Foods but many natural and health food stores carry them. Take the trouble to hunt them down. Once you begin keeping them on hand, you'll never be without them.

Asked for our favorite recipe in the book, we both think almost instantly of a recipe we got from Jennifer English, who hosts the nationally syndicated ABC Wine and Food Network talk show, which chews on great ideas on our subject of choice daily. She told Linda about this fantastic recipe she'd eaten in a Chinese restaurant in Tucson, and explained how to make it over the phone— our idea of kitchen magic for sure when a recipe is that easy. Look for our version of Chinese Tomato Soup; you'll be kissing the Campbell's kids once you learn what a common can of Campbell's original tomato can yield.

behold: the canned soup

1. Chinese Tomato Soup with Shrimp

2. Gazpacho

3. Quick Gazpacho with Bay Shrimp and Cucumber

4. Double-Citrus Black Bean Soup

5. White Bean, Chicken Noodle, and Escarole Soup

6. Canadian Cheese Soup

beautiful boxed soups

1. Butternut Squash Soup with Coriander and Garlic

2. Triple-Ginger Butternut Squash Soup

3. Cream of Spinach and Potato Soup with Sage

4. Potato-Artichoke Soup

5. Seafood Corn Chowder

chinese tomato soup with shrimp

Who knew this old reliable canned tomato soup could become so exotic? Turns out it makes a splendid base for a classic Chinese concoction.

1 tablespoon chili oil

1 cup chopped onion

1 teaspoon chopped garlic

1 (10-ounce) can Campbell's tomato soup

¼ pound frozen peeled and deveined shrimp

¼ cup water chestnuts, drained

1 scallion, minced

½ teaspoon sesame oil

¼ teaspoon ground white pepper

¼ cup frozen peas

Salt

¼ cup minced cilantro

makes 4 servings
time: 20 minutes

1 Sauté onion and garlic.
Heat a medium saucepan over high heat; then add the chili oil and onion. Sauté until the onion is translucent, about 5 minutes. Stir in the garlic, and cook until the garlic begins to brown, about 3 minutes.

2 Make the soup.
Pour the soup and 1 can of water over the garlic and onion mixture. Add the shrimp, water chestnuts, scallion, sesame oil, and white pepper. Boil gently just until shrimp turns pink, 3 to 5 minutes. Stir in the frozen peas and heat through. Season to taste with salt, if needed.

3 Serve.
Ladle into soup bowls, and finish with minced cilantro.

gazpacho

Great for a picnic; add a few ice cubes for an instant winner. Who knew canned tomatoes could be so good?

2	thick slices white or French bread
1	(28-ounce) can whole plum tomatoes and juice
¼	cup extra-virgin olive oil
1	tablespoon white or red wine vinegar (thyme or tarragon vinegar adds additional flavor)
1 to 2	garlic cloves (less if you are averse to garlic)
	Pinch of cayenne
	Freshly milled black pepper
1	teaspoon salt
	Dollop of sour cream (for garnish)
½	green bell pepper or 2 tablespoons parsley, finely chopped (for garnish)

makes 4 to 6 servings
time: 15 minutes

1 Soak the bread.

In a shallow bowl, combine the bread and ½ cup of water, and set it aside until it is mushy.

2 Purée the tomatoes.

Place the tomatoes, olive oil, vinegar, garlic, cayenne, black pepper to taste, and the salt in a blender, and purée for 3 to 5 minutes, or until the consistency is smooth. Add the soaked bread to the blender, and purée it for another minute.

3 Chill and serve.

Add 6 ice cubes to the blender, and stir by hand. Set aside to let the ice cubes melt. Stir in the water, and pour the soup into the serving bowls. Garnish with sour cream and chopped green pepper or parsley.

quick gazpacho with bay shrimp and cucumber

Chill balloon wineglasses, and make sure all ingredients are icy cold before you compose this almost-instant sweet hot gazpacho.

1 **English seedless cucumber**

1 **pound cooked bay shrimp**

1 **quart Clamato tomato cocktail**

Tabasco sauce

makes 4 servings
time: 15 minutes

1 Prepare the cucumber.

Cut the cucumber in half. Peel and dice one half. Cut remaining half into long swizzle sticks. Plunge them into ice water, and hold until serving time.

2 Make the gazpacho.

Toss the diced cucumber with the shrimp. Divide among serving glasses. Pour over icy cold tomato juice, and add a shot of Tabasco to each glass, according to taste. Garnish with cucumber swizzle stick, and serve at once.

double-citrus black bean soup

Black beans are a staple for a quarter of the world's population. And no wonder: they are cheap, delicious, and beautiful. All these ingredients are easy to keep on hand.

1 (15-ounce) can black beans, rinsed and slightly mashed with a fork

1 (15-ounce) can black bean soup

½ cup orange juice (fresh squeezed or from the refrigerator)

½ cup fresh lemon juice

Freshly milled pepper

Sour cream (for garnish)

Chopped scallions (for garnish)

Orange and lemon zest (for garnish)

makes 4 servings
time: 15 minutes

1 Heat the soup.
Combine the beans, black bean soup, orange juice, and lemon juice in a medium-size heavy saucepan. Season with pepper to taste. Bring to a boil, and simmer over medium heat for 15 minutes.

2 Serve.
Ladle into individual bowls, and garnish with a dollop of sour cream, some chopped scallions, and orange and lemon zest or any combination thereof.

white bean, chicken noodle, and escarole soup

Got a can of chicken noodle soup lurking in the back of the pantry? Add some canned white beans and escarole, and it's dinner.

6 cups (1 large head) escarole leaves, washed, stems discarded, and chopped (or 2 boxes frozen spinach)

2 tablespoons extra-virgin olive oil

4 garlic cloves, chopped

½ teaspoon hot red pepper flakes

1 (10-ounce) can homestyle chicken noodle soup

1 (19-ounce) can cannellini beans and juice

Freshly milled pepper

Freshly grated Parmesan cheese (for garnish)

makes 8 servings
time: 30 minutes

1 Cook the greens.

Fill a soup pot three-quarters full with water, and bring it to a boil. Cook the chopped greens until they're tender, about 10 minutes. (Or 2 minutes if using frozen.)

2 Cook the beans.

In a second pot, heat the oil, and cook the garlic over medium heat until barely brown. Toss in the red pepper flakes. Add the soup, 1 can of water, and the beans, and bring to a boil. Add the cooked greens, and stir. Season to taste with pepper.

3 Serve.

Ladle the soup into bowls, and add a sprinkling of Parmesan to each bowl.

canadian cheese soup

This is simple soup from the pantry that is remarkably subtle and satisfying in taste. All you need to complete the meal is a salad and maybe a glass of Chilean merlot.

1 tablespoon butter

1 cup chopped onion

1 medium carrot, finely chopped

1 stalk celery, finely chopped

¼ cup all-purpose flour

2 (13¾-ounce) cans chicken broth

3 cups milk

Salt and freshly milled pepper

Paprika

2 cups shredded Cheddar cheese

makes 6 servings
time: 30 minutes

1 Sauté the vegetables.

Heat the butter in a stewpot over medium heat. Place the onion, carrot, and celery in a food processor with a metal blade, and pulse to chop. Add the chopped vegetables to the pot, and sauté until the onion begins to brown, about 5 minutes. Sprinkle with the flour, and cook and stir until the flour blends with vegetable mixture, about 1 minute.

2 Make the soup.

Deglaze the pan with 1 can of broth, making a thick sauce. Stir in the remaining broth and milk. Cook and stir until the vegetables soften, about 5 minutes. Season to taste with the salt, pepper, and paprika. Remove from the heat, add the cheese, and stir to melt. Serve hot.

butternut squash soup with coriander and garlic

We learned how dynamite the blend of coriander, garlic, and butternut squash is from an Indian cook. This complex flavor combo is a winner and adds an exotic flavor to these wonderful boxes of soup.

1 tablespoon butter

1 tablespoon vegetable oil

2 tablespoons coriander

2 garlic cloves, minced

1 (32-ounce) box Butternut Squash Soup (we love Imagine Naturals Organic Soups)

Freshly milled pepper (for garnish)

makes 4 servings
time: 20 minutes

1 Sauté the seasoning base.

In a medium-size heavy soup pot over medium-high heat, melt the butter together with the vegetable oil. Stir in the coriander, and cook for 2 minutes. Stir in the garlic, and cook for 1 more minute, just until it begins to turn gold.

2 Finish the soup.

Stir in the soup mix, and bring it to a boil. Turn the heat down to low, and simmer for 10 minutes. Spoon into individual bowls, garnish with the pepper, and serve.

triple-ginger butternut squash soup

This makes a fine dish for those in need of something healthy and light. You'll find the boxed soup at better supermarkets and natural foods stores under the brand name Imagine.

1 tablespoon olive oil

1 cup chopped onion

1-inch piece of fresh ginger

1 teaspoon ground ginger

3 tablespoons chopped crystallized ginger

2 (16-ounce) boxes butternut squash soup

Salt

4 teaspoons sour cream

2 scallions, thinly sliced

4 teaspoons chopped salted peanuts

makes 6 servings
time: 15 minutes or less

1 Make the flavor base.

In a soup pot, heat the oil, and sauté the onion over medium heat until golden. Transfer the cooked onions to a food processor. Add the three kinds of ginger, and purée until smooth, adding a little soup as needed to create the purée.

2 Make the soup.

Pour the purée back into the soup pot, and add the remaining boxed soup. Season to taste with salt. Simmer for a few minutes to blend the flavors.

3 Serve.

Pour into soup bowls, top with a dollop of sour cream, sliced scallions, and chopped peanuts.

cream of spinach and potato soup with sage

We learned from a group of northern Italians who came to cook for us one time that spinach and sage are great complements. Pick up fresh sage every other week at the grocery store. It adds an interesting flavor to many otherwise ordinary dishes. Try it in an omelet, in a cream sauce, or in a salad dressing. If you've got the space, pick up a plant and grow it. Grows like a weed, it does.

2 (11-ounce) packages creamed spinach (we like Boston Market brand)

1 (32-ounce) box potato or potato leek soup

¼ cup fresh sage (1 tablespoon dried)

Juice and zest of 1 lemon

Freshly milled pepper

makes 4 servings
time: 15 minutes

1 Combine the ingredients.

In a stock pot or Dutch oven, stir together the creamed spinach, potato soup, sage, lemon juice and zest, and pepper to taste. Heat on medium heat for 5 to 7 minutes, until the soup begins to boil.

2 Simmer.

Reduce the heat to low, and gently simmer the soup for 10 minutes to combine the flavors. Serve hot.

potato-artichoke soup

Straight from the box, the potato-leek soup might remind you of the main fare at the gulag. We have made this stuff a meal simply by adding a few tasty ingredients, all of which can be kept on hand.

1 (8-ounce) package frozen artichoke hearts

2 tablespoons water

1 (15-ounce) can chicken broth

1 (32-ounce) box potato-leek soup (we love Imagine Foods)

1 cup frozen peas

1 garlic clove, minced

½ head romaine lettuce, shredded

Fresh mint sprigs and sour cream (for garnish)

makes 4 servings
time: 15 minutes

1 Thaw the artichoke hearts.

In a large microwavable bowl, combine the artichoke hearts and water, and cook in the microwave on HIGH (100 percent power) for 2 minutes. Drain the artichoke halves, and slice them into quarters.

2 Make the soup.

In a large heavy soup pot or Dutch oven, combine the chicken broth, soup, artichoke hearts, peas, and garlic. Cook over medium-high heat for 10 minutes.

3 Finish the soup.

Stir in the romaine lettuce, and remove from the heat. Serve in individual soup bowls, and garnish with a dollop of sour cream or a sprig of mint. Serve at once.

seafood corn chowder

Corn soup in a box. What a revelation. This silky stuff is perfect for souping up. Here is one delicious way we have found to do so.

3 tablespoons olive oil

1 onion, chopped

1 garlic clove, chopped

1 red bell pepper, chopped

1 cup canned chicken broth (we love the type with roasted garlic)

1 (32-ounce) box creamy sweet corn soup (we recommend one made by Imagine Foods)

1 (16-ounce) bag frozen shrimp or other seafood

1 (8-ounce) package frozen corn

¼ teaspoon cayenne

makes 4 servings
time: 20 minutes

1 Sauté the vegetables.
Coat the bottom of a large heavy soup pot or Dutch oven with the olive oil. Over medium-high heat, sauté the onion, garlic, and red pepper for about 5 minutes, or until softened.

2 Deglaze the pan.
Keeping the heat at medium-high, pour the chicken broth and soup mix into the pan, stirring and scraping up the brown bits from the bottom of the pan.

3 Finish the soup.
Stir in the frozen seafood, corn, and cayenne, and cook for 10 to 15 minutes. Serve at once.

chapter six *
thinking out of the box

Your family will applaud the meals you conjure when you start off with magic boxes of grains, noodles, or baking mixes. The manufacturer has done all the sleight of hand, partially cooking, seasoning, drying, and packaging the means to magnificent meals.

We divide this section into five parts: couscous, rice, ramen noodles, biscuit mix, and corn-bread mix. You'll find new ways to juice up any box that may be lurking on your shelf.

couscous can do it

1. Curried Couscous with Smoked Turkey and Dates

2. Couscous and Lentils with Grilled Pork Tenderloin

3. Couscous, Chicken, Grapes, and Arugula Salad

4. Cumin Lamb Chops on Couscous with Kalamata Olives

Wonderful couscous, used as an ingredient on the desert for thousands of years. It's a form of pasta made of durum wheat that's cooked, seasoned, dried, and broken into granules. In the latest incarnation, you'll find it baffling that something so tasty could result by doing nothing more than pouring boiling water over it, covering it for five minutes or so, and then fluffing it with a fork. What's not to love?

curried couscous with smoked turkey and dates

The moist texture and intense flavor of smoked turkey along with sweet dates is a wonderful foil for curried couscous. You can either spend five minutes making the couscous or sauté a teaspoon of curry powder in butter and stir it into couscous bought ready-made from the deli; both options are embarrassingly easy.

2   tablespoons butter

1   teaspoon Indian curry powder (we love Madras)

1½ cups chicken broth

1   (10-ounce) box couscous

Salt and freshly milled pepper

¾   pound smoked turkey, thinly sliced and cut into bite-size pieces

¾   cup dates, seeded and coarsely chopped

¼   cup chopped scallions

makes 4 servings
time: 20 minutes

1 Make the couscous.

In a medium heavy saucepan with a tight-fitting lid, melt the butter over medium heat. Stir in the curry powder, and, stirring constantly, cook until fragrant, about 1 minute. Stir in the chicken broth and bring to a boil. Stir in the couscous, cover, and remove from the heat. Let stand, covered, for 5 minutes. Adjust the seasonings with the salt and pepper.

2 Arrange the dish.

Toss the turkey and chopped dates together in a serving bowl. Spoon the couscous out onto a platter, and top with the turkey mixture. Top with the scallions. Serve at once.

couscous and lentils with grilled pork tenderloin

Couscous is tasty, but it can be bland; the new seasoned mixes address that situation nicely. Lentils make it a bit heartier. Use a ridged grill pan in the kitchen to quickly cook a pork tenderloin. It's ready in twenty minutes or less, and it looks as if you cooked all day.

1 pound pork tenderloin

1 tablespoon extra-virgin olive oil, plus more for coating tomatoes

2 garlic cloves, smashed

Salt and freshly milled pepper

1 (6.1-ounce) box tomato-lentil flavor couscous

½ cup currants

1 beefsteak tomato, cut into thick slices

Mint leaves, for garnish

makes 4 servings
time: 30 minutes

1 Prepare the meat.
Rub the pork with the oil, garlic, and salt and pepper to taste, and set it aside while the grill heats.

2 Cook the couscous.
Following package directions, cook the couscous along with the currants.

3 Grill the meat and tomato.
Cook the pork for 17 to 20 minutes, turning from time to time, until the meat is brown on all sides and a thermometer inserted into the middle reads 155°F. Dab the tomato slices with oil, salt, and pepper, and grill them, as well, during the last 5 minutes of cooking the pork.

4 Serve.
Mound a serving of couscous in the middle of each dinner plate. Cut the meat into thick slices, and fan them onto the dinner plates alongside a serving of grilled tomato. Garnish with fresh or dried mint, and serve at once.

couscous, chicken, grapes, and arugula salad

The varied textures and flavors in this salad are truly magical. It's a terrific meal by itself. Add chunks of banana or wedges of grapefruit or orange for an interesting twist.

1 (12-ounce) box couscous

½ teaspoon cumin

2 tablespoons fresh parsley leaves

Salt

1 (10-ounce) package cooked carved chicken breast

2 cups red seedless grape halves

½ cup chopped fresh basil

2 tablespoons walnut pieces

¼ cup citrus salad dressing (we like plain old Kraft)

1 bunch arugula, washed and dried well, stems removed, slightly chopped

makes 4 servings
time: 20 minutes

1 Season the couscous.
In a medium bowl, make the couscous according to the package directions. Stir in the cumin and parsley; then add the salt to taste.

2 Make the topping.
In another bowl, toss the chicken with the grapes, basil, and walnuts, and enough salad dressing to moisten.

3 Arrange the salad.
Divide the arugula among 4 plates. Top with a mound of couscous, and then the chicken mixture. Drizzle any remaining dressing over the salads. Serve at once.

cumin lamb chops on couscous with kalamata olives

A box of couscous, some olives, and lamb. It's the Middle East! Lamb chops freeze so well and defrost very quickly in the microwave. They should be a staple for those who have no time and are bored with the run of the mill. Cumin is a natural complement to the lamb's gamey flavor.

makes 4 servings
time: 20 minutes

Couscous

4 baby carrots, finely chopped
1 stalk celery, finely chopped
1½ cups chicken broth
1 (10-ounce) box couscous

Lamb Chops

8 lamb rib chops
1 garlic clove, halved
1 teaspoon cumin
2 tablespoons vegetable oil
½ cup chopped kalamata olives

1 Make the couscous.

In a heavy medium saucepan with a tight-fitting lid, combine the carrots, celery, and chicken broth, and bring to a boil over medium-high heat. Stir in the couscous, remove from the heat, and cover. Let the couscous stand covered while you make the lamb chops.

2 Cook the lamb chops.

Heat a large black skillet for 3 minutes over medium-high heat. Dry the lamb chops, and rub them with the garlic halves and the cumin. Coat the bottom of the pan with the oil, and heat for 1 more minute. Cook the lamb chops for 4 minutes per side, or until cooked to desired level of doneness.

3 Serve the dish.

Pack the couscous into a ½-cup measure, and unmold onto a plate. Arrange 2 lamb chops next to the couscous, and serve at once. Top with the chopped olives.

rice: oh, really?

1. Saffron Rice with Poached Salmon

2. Cheesy Chicken with Wild Rice and Grape Tomatoes

3. Yellow Rice and Broccoli with Shrimp Sauce

4. Creamy Spinach and Cheese Stovetop Casserole with Ham

Lots of manufacturers have come onto the scene with endless permutations of the original seasoned rice-in-a-box touted as the San Francisco treat, but the principle remains the same: what you buy in the box has been cooked, seasoned, and dried. All you have to do is rehydrate it.

We also have a confession to make regarding rice. While we turned our noses up at Minute brand instant rice for all the obvious reasons, either the manufacturer has made great strides in the product or we've gotten so desperate we don't care anymore. Anyway, instant rice finds its way into our larders on a regular basis now, and we use it. You do what you want to. One particular rice product we recommend unreservedly is yellow rice from Goya. This is a seasoned precooked long-grain rice product that goes together in fifteen minutes. It looks good. It tastes good. We like the slightly bitter undercast to the flavor you get from the turmeric. This rice is colorful; it's delicious. We like it.

saffron rice with poached salmon

Both bitter and sweet with saffron and cinnamon, this gorgeous yellow rice dish is made quickly. If you can, snatch up a box of Goya Yellow Rice mix at the market, and just throw in a couple of sticks of cinnamon while it cooks. It's just about as good. Add a poached salmon fillet you found in the deli section, and dinner is yellow and salmon colored. Eat with your eyes first!

1 cup long-grain rice

½ teaspoon kosher salt

2 cinnamon sticks

   Generous pinch of saffron

1 tablespoon butter

8 ounces poached salmon

2 tablespoons minced fresh parsley (for garnish)

makes 4 servings
time: 15 minutes

1 Cook the rice.

In a medium saucepan, combine the rice with 2 cups of water, the salt, cinnamon, saffron, and butter. Bring to a boil, and stir to distribute the saffron. Reduce the heat to low, cover, and cook until all the water is absorbed, about 15 minutes. Stir again, discarding the cinnamon sticks. Place a paper towel over the top of the pan; then place the lid on the pan. Fluff the rice with a fork; then transfer it to a warmed platter. Use saffron rice as a base for this and other chicken dishes.

2 Serve.

Top the rice with the salmon, garnish with the parsley, and serve.

cheesy chicken with wild rice and grape tomatoes

Good enough for company, this dish mainly requires unattended time in the oven when you begin with a box of rice.

4 chicken breast halves on the bone with skin

4 ounces herb-flavored Neufchâtel cheese

Salt and freshly milled pepper

2 teaspoons extra-virgin olive oil

1 pint grape or cherry tomatoes

1 (6-ounce) box wild rice mix

Fresh rosemary needles, for garnish

makes 4 servings
time: 30 minutes

1 Prepare the chicken.

Preheat the oven to 400°F. Spritz a 9 × 13-inch glass baking dish with olive oil cooking spray. Using your fingers, loosen the skin from the breasts. Spread about 2 tablespoons of cheese under the skin of each one. Season to taste with the salt and pepper. Dab the breasts with the olive oil, and arrange them on the baking dish, sides not touching.

2 Bake the chicken.

Cook the chicken on the middle rack of the oven, uncovered, just until the juices run clear and an instant-read thermometer reads 170°F in the thickest part, about 20 minutes. Throw the tomatoes around the chicken during the last 5 minutes of cooking in the oven.

3 Cook the rice.

Following package directions, cook the wild rice mix.

4 Serve.

Arrange a serving of rice on each plate, and top with a chicken breast and a scoop of tomatoes. Garnish with the rosemary, and serve at once.

yellow rice and broccoli
with shrimp sauce

Canned shrimp soup is a tried-and-true staple for a fast, flavorful meal. Serve this colorful layered dinner—yellow, green, and pink—on a dark blue plate, and it's a feast for the eyes, too. Don't have any shrimp handy? Substitute fully cooked chicken breast. Can't find shrimp soup? Substitute cream of chicken. Just keep in mind that these soups are salty, so you'll probably only need to add pepper and perhaps a squirt of citrus juice to balance out the flavors.

1   (8-ounce) package yellow rice

3   cups water

    Salt

1   tablespoon butter or olive oil

1   (10¾-ounce) can cream of shrimp soup

1   (4-ounce) package cream cheese with chives

¼   cup milk or half-and-half

1   scallion, finely chopped

    Juice and zest of ½ lemon

1   cup fresh or frozen cooked and peeled shrimp

    Cayenne

2   (10-ounce) packages fresh or frozen broccoli florets

2   tablespoons, slivered almonds, toasted

makes 4 servings
time: 25 minutes or less

1 Cook the rice.

In a medium saucepan, combine the rice and water. Add a dash of salt and the butter. Cover, and cook until all the liquid is absorbed, about 25 minutes.

2 Make the sauce.

Stir together the soup, cream cheese, milk, scallions, and lemon juice and zest in a medium saucepan. Bring to a simmer over medium-low heat. Add the shrimp, reserving a couple for a garnish. Adjust the seasonings with cayenne.

3 Cook the broccoli.

Microwave or steam the broccoli over boiling water just until tender, about 5 minutes.

4 Serve.

Spoon cooked rice and broccoli onto warmed dinner plates, spoon sauce over, and garnish with the reserved shrimp and slivered almonds.

creamy spinach and cheese
stovetop casserole with
ham

Back to the 1950s for a casserole, except this one is ready to eat in fifteen minutes and can be made on the stove using frozen creamed spinach and the newest incarnation of the quick rice packets—whichever one you have on hand. We used a Lipton rice-and-butter-sauce mix ready in ten minutes. Don't have rice at all? Substitute pasta or whatever's handy. June Cleaver would have been proud.

1 (4.3-ounce) package long-grain rice-and-pasta mix

2 tablespoons extra-virgin olive oil

½ cup chopped onion

1 garlic clove, minced

1 cup red bell pepper cut into matchstick julienne

4 ounces fully cooked ham steak, cut into julienne strips

1 (10-ounce) package frozen creamed spinach

½ cup cream or milk

Salt and freshly milled pepper

¼ cup grated sharp Cheddar cheese

makes 4 to 6 servings
time: 15 minutes

1 Cook the rice.
Following package directions, cook the rice and pasta until tender, about 10 minutes.

2 Make the sauce.
In a heavy saucepan, heat the oil over medium-high heat, and sauté the onion and garlic until the onion becomes translucent; then add the red pepper and ham, and continue to cook until the pepper begins to lose its shape, about 3 minutes. Add the frozen creamed spinach and cream, cover, and heat until the spinach is hot throughout.

3 Finish the casserole.
Stir to mix the sauce; then stir in the cooked rice mixture. Cover, and reheat. Adjust the seasonings with the salt and pepper. Top with the cheese, cover, and set aside until ready to serve.

friends, ramens, countrymen

1. **Sweet and Tangy Ramen Salad**

2. **Salmon Ramen with Creamy Carrots and Cabbage**

3. **Noodle Strudel with Chicken**

4. **Spinach Ramen Salad**

5. **Ramen Pizza with Portobellos and Pepperoni**

6. **Cold Sesame Ramen Noodles**

How many passages into adulthood were fueled by that old standby from our youth, ramen noodles. By now, an entire generation has lived to tell the tale. Top Ramen is delicious. And that little bag of seasoning can either be used in the recipe or tossed depending on how much salt and MSG you can tolerate. Add a few choice extras and it's dinner fit for an emperor.

sweet and tangy ramen salad

How many boomers fueled their passage into adulthood with Top Ramen—ten for a dollar. Somewhere along the line we heard these cheap eats were unhealthy and loaded with fat. What a loss. Then we heard about the not-fried-to-death noodles called chuka soba. *They're about a dollar a package instead of a dime, but they're just as fast, and the resulting salad tastes great.*

Dressing

makes 4 servings
time: 20 minutes

- ¼ cup rice vinegar
- ¼ teaspoon sugar
- 2 tablespoons honey
- 1 tablespoon vegetable oil
- 1 tablespoon soy sauce
- Salt and freshly ground black pepper
- Pinch of cayenne

Salad

- 1 (5-ounce) package Japanese curly noodles (*chuka soba*)
- 4 cups shredded napa cabbage
- 1 carrot, grated
- 2 scallions, cut on the diagonal into ½-inch pieces
- ½ cup sunflower seed kernels or slivered almonds
- 10 ounces (2 cups) sliced cooked chicken breast from a rotisserie bird or roasted sliced chicken breast

1 Make the dressing.

Pour the vinegar, sugar, honey, oil, soy sauce, salt and black pepper to taste, and the cayenne into a 2-cup glass measure. Heat in the microwave on HIGH (100 percent power) to boiling, about 1 minute.

2 Make the salad.

Crumble the noodles into a large salad bowl. Add the warm dressing, and let stand for 10 minutes. Add the cabbage, carrot, scallions, and sunflower seeds and toss to coat. Arrange the chicken slices on top.

3 Serve.

Serve the salad immediately on chilled plates, or cover and refrigerate for up to 8 hours.

salmon ramen with creamy carrots and cabbage

Aromatic dill, succulent salmon, and plain old ramen in a creamy sauce makes for dinner magic. Don't have fresh salmon? Substitute a ten-ounce can, drained.

2 (5-ounce) packages Japanese curly noodles (*chuka soba*)

1 (8-ounce) salmon side, cut into 4 pieces

2 tablespoons unsalted butter

1 cup chopped onion

¾ cup cream or milk

4 ounces cream cheese

1 teaspoon dried dill

1 cup whole baby carrots

1 cup shredded cabbage

makes 4 servings
time: 20 minutes

1 Prepare the salmon.

Open the noodle flavoring packet, and rub the seasoning into the salmon side. In a large skillet, heat the butter over medium heat; then sauté the onion and salmon for about 5 minutes, just until the onion is clear and the salmon is cooked on both sides, turning only once. Remove the salmon to a plate, and keep it warm.

2 Make the sauce.

Pour the cream into the skillet. Pinch off pieces of cream cheese, and add them to the milk. Cook and stir until the sauce is smooth. Add the dill, carrots, and cabbage, and cook until the carrots are tender, about 5 minutes. Add cream or milk as needed to maintain a gravylike consistency.

3 Cook the noodles.

Meanwhile, in a separate pot, bring 3 cups of water to a boil, and cook the noodles for 3 minutes. Drain; then stir the noodles into the veggie mixture.

4 Serve.

Ladle into soup bowls, place salmon pieces on top, and garnish with additional dill.

noodle strudel with chicken

China meets Germany over Japanese noodles in an American kitchen with a Hawaiian pineapple sauce. Is this what they mean by "one world"? We just call it good.

2 (5-ounce) packages Japanese curly noodles (*chuka soba*)

1 large egg, lightly beaten

1 teaspoon sesame oil

Salt and freshly milled pepper

1 (10-ounce) package cooked carved chicken breast

1 cup chopped red bell pepper

1 cup broccoli florets

1 (8-ounce) can crushed pineapple in light syrup

1 tablespoon packed brown sugar

1 tablespoon rice wine vinegar

2 teaspoons cornstarch

2 tablespoons almond slivers

makes 4 servings
time: 30 minutes

1 Cook the noodles.

In a medium saucepan, bring 3 cups of water to a boil, and cook the noodles for 3 minutes. Drain. Mix in the beaten egg and sesame oil.

2 Make the strudel.

Preheat the oven to 350°F. Spritz a 10-inch square baking dish with cooking spray. Arrange half the cooked noodles in the bottom, and season generously with the salt and pepper. Layer with the chicken, ¾ cup of the bell pepper, and ¾ cup of the broccoli.

3 Make the sauce.

In a medium saucepan, combine the noodle seasoning, pineapple and juice, sugar, vinegar, and cornstarch. Cook and stir until thick and glossy, about 3 minutes. Pour half the sauce over the first layer of strudel.

4 Bake the strudel.

Add the remaining noodles, and pour the sauce over all. Finish with almond slivers. Bake for 20 minutes. Garnish with the reserved broccoli and red pepper.

5 Serve.

Let the strudel stand on the sideboard for 3 or 4 minutes; then cut it into squares, and serve.

spinach ramen salad

For ease in eating, break the dry noodles into the boiling water. Then all you have to do is compose the salad from its sweet, salty, bitter, sour, and crunchy parts. Pure magic.

2 (5-ounce) packages Japanese curly noodles (*chuka soba*)

1 (10-ounce) package triple-washed baby spinach

1 (6-ounce) piece poached salmon

1 cup red or green seedless grapes

1 cup red bell pepper, finely diced

½ cup cashew nuts

½ cup crumbled Gorgonzola

makes 4 servings
time: 20 minutes

Dressing

2 flavor packets from the noodles

3 garlic cloves, minced

Grated zest and 3 tablespoons juice of 1 lemon

⅓ cup extra-virgin olive oil

¼ cup mayonnaise

1 lemon cut into wedges (for garnish)

1 Cook the noodles.

In a medium saucepan, bring 3 cups of water to a boil, and cook the noodles for 3 minutes. Drain and cool completely.

2 Make the salad.

Toss the cooked noodles with the spinach, salmon pieces, grapes, pepper, cashews, and cheese.

3 Make the dressing.

Combine the dressing ingredients in a jar, and shake to mix; then drizzle as needed over the salad.

4 Serve.

Divide the salad immediately among 4 dinner plates, garnished with the lemon wedges.

ramen pizza with
portobellos and pepperoni

Dorm food goes uptown. Meaty portobellos sliced thin taste as good as steak. Want a change? Substitute frozen Italian meatballs for pepperoni. Wanna be a vegetarian? You know what to do.

2 (5-ounce) packages Japanese curly noodles (*chuka soba*)

3 cups water

3 ounces pepperoni, thinly sliced

2 cups sliced portobello mushrooms

2 tablespoons extra-virgin olive oil

1 cup prepared pasta sauce

8 ounces fresh mozzarella cheese, cut into thick slices

3 ounces freshly grated Parmesan cheese

makes 4 servings
time: 20 minutes

1 Prepare the pan.

Preheat the oven to 350°F. Spritz a deep-dish pizza pan with cooking spray.

2 Cook the noodles.

In a medium saucepan, bring 3 cups of water to a boil, and cook the noodles for 3 minutes. Drain. Arrange the cooked noodles in the prepared pan. Top with the pepperoni and mushrooms. Moisten the pizza with the olive oil. Pour spaghetti sauce over it, then top with mozzarella and Parmesan.

3 Bake the pizza.

Bake until golden and bubbly, about 20 minutes. Cool on a rack for 5 minutes; then cut into wedges, and serve.

cold sesame ramen noodles

Mixing peanut butter and ramen noodles is, quite simply, down-home wizardry. Think of it as putting something ordinary into a top hat, covering that hat with a red silk scarf, whisking off the scarf—and up fly the white doves!

2 (5-ounce) packages Japanese curly noodles (*chuka soba*)

1 cup scallions, cut on the bias into 1-inch pieces

makes 4 servings
time: 20 minutes

Sauce

⅓ cup chunky peanut butter

2 tablespoons peanut oil

2 tablespoons sesame oil

½ teaspoon sugar

2 tablespoons soy sauce

2 tablespoons rice wine vinegar

2 tablespoons water

2 teaspoons chili fermented black bean paste

2 tablespoons black sesame seeds

1 Cook the noodles.

In a medium saucepan, bring 3 cups of water to a boil, and cook the noodles for 3 minutes. Drain, and toss with the scallions.

2 Make the sauce.

Meanwhile, stir together the peanut butter and oils until well blended; then add the sugar, soy, vinegar, water, and chili paste (use less or more paste, as you desire). Whisk until you have an emulsion; then fold the sauce into the cooked noodles. Cover and refrigerate until serving time.

3 Serve.

Divide the noodles among 4 dinner plates, and top with the black sesame seeds.

biscuits, bountiful biscuits

1. Pennsylvania Dutch Chicken-Dill Potpies

2. Sage Buttermilk Biscuits with Sausage, Shirred Eggs, and Cheddar

3. Southwestern Tamale Tart with Black Beans

4. Root Vegetable Cobbler with Chive Biscuit Topping

5. Ham and Succotash Stew with Cheddar Biscuits

The comfort food of the 1950s has made a soaring comeback in our society. Want to make people in your household feel better? Want to create enchantment at the dinner table? Most anything you can make and top with biscuits makes it look as if you really knocked yourself out. Use a biscuit mix. It's quick. And once again, where we live, you can actually buy decent biscuits already made and put up in plastic at the high-end grocery store. So if you're already pinned to the wall with duties, skip over the biscuit-making part altogether, and grab a bag of premade biscuits. In recipes you'll find in this section, they work admirably.

One caveat about biscuits and shortbreads of any kind: Unlike other breads, they have a short life. They're always best if made and eaten the same day. Don't buy biscuits and put them aside for a week and then think you can use them for anything besides feeding the birds. Two days out, and they're gone. Trust us on this. We know from bitter, disappointing experience.

To get the best results when working with a biscuit mix or baking and quick bread mixes, be sure to

1. Measure accurately. Spoon the baking mix into the measure lightly. Don't sift or pack it. Level with the edge of a knife.

2. Measure liquids using a glass measure, looking carefully to see that you don't have too much or too little.

3. Use only large eggs for best results.

4. For a tender result, don't overmix the batter. Stir just until all the ingredients are well moistened. About fifty strokes should do it.

5. Use the correct pan size. Too big a pan, and you'll get a flat result. Too small, and it may run over in the oven.

6. Keep a thermometer in your oven for accuracy. Most oven thermostats get off after a while, and an independent thermometer is the simplest way to make adjustments.

7. Thoroughly preheat the oven, and place the rack in the middle. Place the cake in the center of that rack.

8. Bake just until the cake is golden brown and a toothpick inserted into the middle comes out clean.

9. Cool the cake on a rack for 5 to 10 minutes before cutting to let the starches settle down. Cut too soon, the hot cake may seem doughy and a bit like bubble gum.

pennsylvania dutch chicken-dill potpies

If you've ever been to Reading Terminal Market in downtown Philadelphia, you will have seen the Amish vendors from around Lancaster, Pennsylvania, some of the world's great farm cooks. Buy a chicken potpie from one of them, and you begin to get an idea of this pure farmland way of life. You can get a fair approximation in your own kitchen by starting with a roast chicken and a box of Bisquick. Bake it in one large casserole dish, or for maximum drama, place the contents in individual ramekins so that everybody gets his own individual pie, with the aroma of vegetables and chicken wafting up through a dill-scented biscuit.

Buttermilk Dill Biscuits

makes 6 servings
time: about 30 minutes

- 2 cups biscuit mix
- 1 teaspoon dill
- 2 tablespoons fresh minced parsley
- ½ cup buttermilk

Chicken Potpie Filling

- 2 tablespoons butter
- ½ cup finely chopped red bell pepper
- ½ cup chopped onion
- ¾ teaspoon thyme
- 1 cup chopped brown mushrooms
- 5 tablespoons all purpose flour
- 1 (16-ounce) bag frozen mixed root vegetables
- 1 (15-ounce) can chicken broth
- ½ cup heavy cream
  Salt and freshly milled pepper
- 1 (2- to 3-pound) rotisserie chicken, skinned, boned, and chopped

1 Make the biscuits.

Combine the biscuit mix with the dill and parsley, blending well. Add the buttermilk, and stir with a fork to moisten. Remove the batter to a board lightly sprinkled with biscuit mix. Knead two or three times; then pat out into a ½-inch-thick circle. For individual ramekins, cut into six pieces to fit your dishes. For a larger pie, set the dough circle aside, as is.

2 Make the filling.

In a large skillet over medium-high heat, heat the butter, and sauté the pepper and onion until the onion turns golden, about 5 minutes, adding the thyme and mushrooms after 2 minutes. Sprinkle with the flour. Cook and stir until the flour begins to brown, about 3 minutes. Add the vegetables and broth, and stir to mix. Cook until thick, about 5 minutes; then finish with the cream. Season to taste with salt and pepper. Add the chicken and toss to mix.

3 Bake the pies.

Preheat the oven to 450°F. Spritz either 6 individual 2-cup ramekins or soufflé dishes or 1 large casserole with vegetable oil cooking spray. Spoon in the filling. Top with the biscuit dough. Bake until the filling is bubbling and the biscuits are puffed and brown, 12 to 16 minutes. Let stand for 5 minutes before serving.

sage buttermilk biscuits
with sausage, shirred eggs, and cheddar

No matter what time you like your breakfast—morning, noon, or night—this all-in-one dish is welcome. Choose clever little ramekins to serve it in if you have them, plain old Pyrex baking dishes if you don't. The idea is that you make a three-layer dish that gets baked together. This is a handy dish to serve for brunch, when a number of people show up and you'd rather visit with them than kill yourself cooking.

Sage Buttermilk Biscuits

makes 10 to 12 servings
time: 30 minutes

- 2 cups biscuit mix
- 2 tablespoons finely chopped fresh sage (or 2 teaspoons dried, crumbled)
- ¼ cup grated sharp Cheddar cheese
- ½ cup buttermilk

Sausage and Egg Filling

- 1 pound bulk fresh pork sausage (we like Jimmy Dean)
- 10 large eggs

1 Make the biscuits.

Combine the biscuit mix with the sage and cheese, blending well. Add the buttermilk, and stir with a fork to moisten. Remove the batter to a board lightly sprinkled with biscuit mix. Knead two or three times; then pat out into a ½-inch-thick circle. Cut into ten pieces to fit your ramekins, and set aside.

2 Cook the sausage.

Cut the sausage into 10 equal pieces, and flatten them into 3-inch rounds. Cook the sausage in 2 batches in a large skillet over medium heat, turning, until cooked through, about 8 minutes. Drain on paper towels.

3 Bake the dish.

Preheat the oven to 350°F. Spritz 10 ramekins with vegetable oil cooking spray. Add a piece of cooked sausage to the bottom of each dish. Break an egg into each one. Add a "hat" of biscuit dough, laying it on gently so as not to break the egg yolk. Bake until the biscuits are brown, about 15 minutes. Serve hot.

southwestern tamale tart with black beans

Do you have a tart pan with a removable bottom? That is the easiest container in which to make this gorgeous tart. Don't own one? Use a 9-inch pie plate. Then you have a pie instead of a tart, but either way you get the glories of chiles, corn, beans, and tomatoes.

<table>
<tr><td>1</td><td>cup biscuit mix</td></tr>
<tr><td>½</td><td>cup cornmeal</td></tr>
<tr><td>1½</td><td>cups shredded Cheddar cheese</td></tr>
<tr><td>1</td><td>(4-ounce) can chopped green chiles, drained</td></tr>
<tr><td>⅓</td><td>cup canned beef consommé (or broth)</td></tr>
<tr><td>1</td><td>(15-ounce) can black beans, rinsed and drained</td></tr>
<tr><td>½</td><td>cup chopped cilantro</td></tr>
<tr><td>6</td><td>grape tomatoes, halved</td></tr>
<tr><td></td><td>Salsa, sour cream, and guacamole (for garnish)</td></tr>
</table>

makes 6 servings
time: 45 minutes

1 Prepare the pan.

Preheat the oven to 350°F. Spritz a 10-inch round springform tart pan (or a 9-inch pie pan) with vegetable oil cooking spray, and set it aside.

2 Make the tart.

Combine the biscuit mix, cornmeal, 1 cup of the shredded cheese, and the chiles thoroughly. Stir in the beef consommé. Pat the mixture evenly into the bottom of the pan. Mix the beans and cilantro, and spoon them over the corn-meal mixture to within ½ inch of the edge. Sprinkle with the remaining cheese.

3 Bake the tart.

Bake the tart for 30 to 35 minutes, or until the tart is cooked through. Remove the pan to a rack. Loosen the sides of the tart pan, and remove them. Arrange tomato halves around the edge of the tart. Cut the tart into wedges, and serve with salsa, sour cream, and guacamole.

root vegetable cobbler with
chive biscuit topping

Here's comfort food for the vegetarians of your acquaintance. The aroma of root vegetables when wafting into a baking biscuit would make the most avid meat-eater ravenous. We've cast a spell on the carnivores in our houses with this dish whenever we just don't want another meaty meal.

Biscuit Topping

makes 6 to 8 servings
time: 30 minutes

2 cups biscuit mix

¼ cup fresh snipped chives (or 2 tablespoons dried)

½ cup buttermilk

2 large eggs, beaten

Root Vegetable Filling

3 tablespoons butter

1 cup chopped onion

1 pound potatoes, peeled and cut into ½-inch pieces (about 3 cups)

1 cup baby carrots

1½ teaspoons thyme

1 (14½-ounce) can vegetable broth

1 cup chopped button mushrooms

1 cup frozen peas

¼ cup chopped fresh chives (or 2 tablespoons dried)

1 tablespoon all-purpose flour

Salt and freshly milled black pepper to taste

1 Make the biscuits.

Combine the biscuit mix with the chives, blending well. Add the buttermilk and eggs, and stir with a fork to moisten. Remove the batter to a board lightly sprinkled with biscuit mix. Knead two or three times; then pat out into a ½-inch-thick circle. Cut the dough into 6 3½-inch rounds. Set them aside.

2 Make the filling.

In a large skillet, melt the butter over medium-high heat. Add the onion, and sauté until it turns a deep golden color, about 7 minutes. Add the potatoes, carrots, and thyme. Sauté for about 3 more minutes. Add the broth, mushrooms, and peas. Cook for 3 minutes. Add the chives. Dissolve the flour in a little water, and stir it in. Cook until the filling is thick, adjusting the seasonings with the salt and pepper, 5 to 8 more minutes.

3 Bake the cobbler.

Preheat the oven to 425°F. Spritz 6 ramekins or 1 (3-quart) casserole dish with vegetable oil cooking spray. Divide the filling among the dishes or pour it all into 1 large dish, and top with the biscuits. Don't worry if some filling shows around the edges. That's okay. Place the dishes on a baking sheet, and bake until the topping is golden and the vegetable mixture is heated through, 15 to 18 minutes. Let it stand for 5 minutes, and serve.

ham and succotash stew
with cheddar biscuits

Shades of the Narragansets who mixed corn and lima beans into succotash. No doubt their Pilgrim guests threw in a little ham. This is comfort, pure comfort.

Stew

makes 6 servings
time: 35 minutes

- 2 tablespoons butter
- 1 cup chopped onion
- 2 garlic cloves, smashed
- ¾ pound ham steak, cut into 1-inch pieces (about 2 cups)
- 1 cup baby carrots
- 2 cups (1-pound package) frozen corn
- 2 cups (1-pound package) frozen baby lima beans
- 1 (15-ounce) can chicken broth
- ¾ cup water
- ½ teaspoon thyme
- Salt and freshly milled pepper

Cheddar Buttermilk Biscuits

- 2 cups biscuit mix
- ½ cup grated sharp Cheddar cheese
- ½ cup buttermilk

1 Make the stew.

In a large stew pot over medium-high heat, heat the butter, then sauté the onion until golden, about 5 minutes, adding the garlic in the last minute. Add the ham steak, carrots, corn, and lima beans. Cook, stirring, for 3 minutes, then pour in the broth and water. Add the thyme. Simmer for about 15 minutes, then season with the salt and pepper.

2 Make the biscuits.

Combine the biscuit mix with the cheese, blending well. Add the buttermilk, and stir with a fork to moisten. Remove the batter to a board lightly sprinkled with biscuit mix. Knead two or three times; then pat out into a ½-inch-thick circle. Divide the dough into 6 (3½-inch) rounds. Set them aside.

3 Bake the stew.

Preheat the oven to 425°F. Spritz a large baking dish with vegetable oil cooking spray. Add the stew to the dish. Top with the biscuits. Bake until the biscuits are golden, about 15 minutes. Cool for 5 minutes; then serve in soup bowls.

corn bread in a jiffy

In the teeth of the Great Depression, 1930 to be exact, Mable White Holmes created the first Jiffy corn-bread mix. She claimed then, "This mix is so simple, even a man can do it." Write that down. Little did she know how far a half-scratch magician could take that humble little box.

Our pantries always hold a few boxes of Jiffy, right beside the ever-present cake mixes, so we're covered, and you can be, too. It's easy, it's foolproof, and it's fun to make stuff with a box of Jiffy, from sensational starters to hearty main courses.

And if you're too far gone to pull off even preparing corn bread, go ahead and buy the corn bread. Yes, buy it. We see it for sale every week. Do we buy it? Please, no. We are under the illusion that we're cooking so long as that golden aroma of baking corn bread comes wafting from our own kitchens. But what you do in your kitchen is up to you, and a good magician never reveals his secrets.

1. **Johnnycakes with Bay Scallops**

2. **Mini Corn Muffins with Ham and Honey Mustard**

3. **Pepper Corn Bread**

4. **Arkansas Corn Casserole**

5. **Texas Beefy Casserole**

6. **Grandmama's Scalloped Corn and Tomatoes**

7. **Strictly for the Birds Corn Bread**

johnnycakes with bay scallops

Nothing like a few boxes of Jiffy corn-bread mix in the pantry for brunch in a hurry. Serve these crisp corn cakes from morning to night to grateful diners, especially when you want to make a midday meal special. Fresh out of scallops? Use crumbled bacon instead.

1	(8½-ounce) package corn-bread mix
¼	teaspoon sea salt
¼	pound bay scallops (or 4 bacon strips cooked and chopped)
¼	cup corn kernels, fresh or frozen
1	large egg
¾	cup buttermilk
2	teaspoons minced roasted red pepper
1	scallion, minced
2	tablespoons melted butter
	Vegetable oil cooking spray for the griddle

makes 4 servings
time: 25 minutes

1 Make the batter.

In a large bowl, stir the corn-bread mix and salt. Add the scallops and corn to the mixture, and toss to combine. In a smaller bowl, whisk together the egg, buttermilk, red pepper, scallion, and melted butter. Pour the egg mixture over the cornmeal mixture, and stir to mix thoroughly.

2 Cook the johnnycakes.

Heat a large nonstick griddle or skillet over medium heat. Coat the bottom with vegetable oil cooking spray. Preheat the oven to 225°F. Using 2 tablespoons, drop the batter onto the hot skillet, and cook until the edges begin to brown. Flip the johnnycakes over, and brown the other side. Transfer the cooked cakes to a platter, and keep them warm in the preheated oven. Reheat the skillet, and cook another batch. While you make the remaining johnnycakes, serve these hot, with maple syrup for breakfast, brunch, or a fast supper.

mini corn muffins with ham and honey mustard

Mini muffins have become a regular at any grocery store. They make a perfect base for a brightly flavored and colored hors d'oeuvres. Can't find them? Buy a box of Jiffy, and make your own. Just remember to put paper liners in those muffin tins, or you'll drive yourself crazy washing the pan.

½ cup honey

¾ cup mustard

3 dozen mini corn muffins from the bakery, sliced horizontally

1 pound ham, thinly sliced

makes 12 servings
time: 15 minutes

1 Make the spread.
Mix the honey and mustard thoroughly.

2 Fill the muffins.
Spread each muffin generously with the spread, and place a slice of ham between the layers. Cover them until you are ready to serve.

pepper corn bread

For a quick accompaniment to soups or casseroles, doctor up a box of corn-bread mix with cracked black pepper. Doesn't take a minute, and it kicks up the flavor.

1 (8½-ounce) package Jiffy corn-muffin mix

1 large egg

⅓ cup buttermilk

1 teaspoon cracked black pepper

makes 6 servings
time: 20 minutes

1 Prepare to bake.
Preheat the oven to 400°F. Spritz an 8-inch square baking pan.

2 Make the batter and bake.
In a medium bowl, blend all the ingredients. The batter will be slightly lumpy. Let the batter rest for 3 or 4 minutes; then pour it into the prepared baking pan. Bake until golden brown, 15 to 20 minutes.

3 Serve.
Cool on a rack, and cut into squares. Best if it's served the day it's made.

arkansas corn casserole

Here's a recipe from a high-profile celebrity who would rather it not be known that she's ever been inside a kitchen except to instruct the cook. She actually knows how to make this. Throw in some cooked ham or crumbled bacon if you wish. This is down-home cooking at its best. It's what Ms. Celeb makes on cook's night out.

4 tablespoons (½ stick) butter

1 red bell pepper, chopped

½ onion, chopped

2 large eggs

1 (10-ounce) can cream-style corn

1 (8-ounce) can whole kernel corn, drained

1 (8-ounce) box Jiffy corn-bread mix

8 ounces sour cream

1 cup shredded Cheddar cheese

Paprika (for garnish)

makes 4 to 6 servings
time: 45 minutes

1 Prepare the vegetables.

In a skillet over medium heat, sauté the onion and bell pepper in butter until the onion begins to brown, about 5 minutes.

2 Mix the casserole.

Preheat the oven to 325°F. Spritz a 3-quart casserole dish with vegetable oil cooking spray. In a medium bowl combine the eggs, corn, and corn-bread mix. Mix in the sautéed vegetables, and pour the whole thing into the prepared casserole dish. Spread sour cream on top, add cheese, and sprinkle with paprika. Bake until brown and bubbly on top, about 40 minutes.

texas beefy casserole

A meal-in-one made even easier using fully cooked beef crumbles and Jiffy corn-bread mix. Only have hamburger meat? Cook it along with the onions, and go forth.

¾ cup chopped onion

1 tablespoon olive oil

3 tablespoons flour

1 cup cream or milk

⅔ cup water

1 pound chili-seasoned fully cooked ground beef crumbles

Salt and freshly milled pepper

1 (8-ounce) package Jiffy corn-bread mix

1 egg

1 cup frozen peas (we like Green Giant)

makes 4 to 6 servings
time: 35 minutes

1 Make the sauce.

In a large skillet, sauté the onion in oil over medium heat. Stir in the flour, and cook until the flour begins to brown, about 3 minutes. Pour in the cream and water. Cook, stirring, until thickened. Add the cooked beef, and season to taste with salt and pepper.

2 Prepare the casserole.

Spritz a 3-quart casserole dish with vegetable oil cooking spray. Preheat the oven to 400°F. Prepare the corn-bread mix, following the package directions, and incorporating the egg as instructed.

3 Finish the casserole.

Pour the meat mixture into the prepared casserole dish. Top with a layer of peas. Then top with the corn-bread batter, dropped on by the spoonful. Don't worry if every inch isn't covered. Let some peas peek through. Bake until the corn bread is brown, about 25 minutes.

4 Serve.

Cool on a rack for 10 minutes; then scoop it onto plates.

grandmama's scalloped corn and tomatoes

Who says grandmothers have to cook from scratch? Not our Grandnonnie! She thought any recipe could be made better if you just added a little Cool Whip to the ingredient list. We're not going to do it this time, you understand, but the principle remains. Take every shortcut you can. If it's made with love, people will love it.

1 (16-ounce) can creamed corn

1 (16-ounce) can Mexican-style corn, drained

1 (8-ounce) can chopped tomatoes and juice

½ cup butter, softened

1 tablespoon packed brown sugar

4 large eggs, lightly beaten

2 (8-ounce) boxes Jiffy corn-bread mix

2 cups sour cream

makes 8 servings
time: 50 minutes

1 Make the casserole.

Preheat the oven to 375°F. Spritz a 9 × 13-inch baking dish with vegetable oil cooking spray. In a large bowl, combine the cans of corn, the tomatoes, butter, sugar, eggs, corn-bread mix, and 1 cup of the sour cream. Mix, then transfer to the prepared baking dish. Top the mixture with the remaining sour cream.

2 Bake the casserole.

Place the casserole on the middle rack of the preheated oven, and bake until it's golden brown on top, about 45 minutes. Cool on a rack. Cut into squares, and serve warm.

strictly for the birds corn bread

We're not kidding. This half-scratch magic is for our feathered friends. We make it for finches when the snow is on the ground. Are they grateful? They don't issue even one squawk if you cheat and start with a mix. Don't be surprised if the blue jays make off with most of it. They love it, too.

1 (8-ounce) box Jiffy corn-bread mix
1 dozen large eggs with shells
½ cup wheat germ
¼ cup powdered milk
1 tablespoon poppy seeds
1 teaspoon bird vitamins*

makes enough to feed
50 or 60 finches
time: 35 minutes

1 Make the batter.
Preheat the oven to 350°F. Spritz a 9 × 13-inch glass baking dish with vegetable oil cooking spray. In a large bowl, stir together the corn-bread mix, eggs (reserve the shells), wheat germ, milk, and poppy seeds. Mix until smooth; then transfer to the prepared baking dish.

2 Bake the bread.
Bake until a toothpick inserted in the center comes out clean, 20 to 25 minutes. The top will be quite brown.

3 Bake the eggshells.
While the corn bread is baking, prepare the eggshells. Lay them out one layer deep on a dry baking sheet. Pop them into the oven until they begin to turn brown, 10 to 20 minutes. Cool, then reduce to a rough grind in a food processor.

* Bird vitamins are sold in pet stores or the pet section of your supermarket.

4 Make the birdfeed.

When the corn bread is cool, break it into the food processor bowl, and process until it's got a crumbly consistency. Mix it with the ground eggshells and bird vitamins. Freeze the mixture in small sandwich baggies so that you can feed it to your birdies over the cold winter.

5 Thaw and feed.

Remove each baggie to the refrigerator overnight; then spread on the bird feeder.

part three
vanishing act: desserts that disappear

Sometimes, for no reason at all, just as a spur of the moment thing, nothing will quite do like a homemade dessert.

But we don't want some complicated procedure that's going to eat up our Saturday. We don't want seventeen steps that result in two dishwasher loads of bowls and pans. We don't want anything that's not quite as good as what we could buy at the bakery.

Homemade dessert must be memorable. It must taste good and look good and not kill the cook to make it. The desserts that follow fit the bill to a tee.

chapter seven *
cakes that start in a box

Yes, we're all too busy. Yes, we're all swamped and have no time. And yet children's birthdays, office celebrations, and anniversaries still come around, as sure as the sun rises in the East. And what do we want to celebrate with?

We want cake. A fine, festive cake that looks gorgeous and tastes divine. And we want to say, "I made it myself."

But if it started with a mix, who's the wiser?

1. **Italian Lemon Chiffon Cake**

2. **Pineapple–Macadamia Nut Cake with Four-Minute Coconut Frosting**

3. **Cinnamon-Apple Pound Cake with a Cider Sauce**

4. **Butter-Pecan Rum-Soaked Sheet Cake**

5. **Berry-Spice Swirl Cake**

6. **Warm Lemon Cake**

7. **Chocolate-Bourbon Bundt Cake**

8. **Tropical Torte with Coconut, Pineapple, and Pistachio Nuts**

9. **Meredith Pollak's Rum Cake**

10. **Banana-Nut Bundt Cake**

italian lemon chiffon cake

Count on the Italians to have the secret. Choose extra-virgin olive oil for the cake, and you've pumped up the flavor. Use a chiffon method, and you get a cake as light as a cloud, as piquant as a love affair.

1 tablespoon all-purpose flour

5 large eggs, divided

½ teaspoon cream of tartar

1 (18.5-ounce) package yellow cake mix

¾ cup fresh lemon juice

¼ cup water

¼ cup extra-virgin olive oil

1 teaspoon grated lemon zest

makes 16 servings
time: 50 minutes

Lemon Glaze

1 cup confectioners' sugar

3 tablespoons fresh lemon juice (or more as needed)

1 teaspoon lemon zest cut into long curls (for garnish)

1 Prepare the pan.

Spritz a 10-inch tube pan or Bundt cake pan with vegetable oil cooking spray. Sprinkle with flour, and coat all surfaces. Tap out excess flour, and set the pan aside. Preheat the oven to 350°F.

2 Beat the eggs.

Place the 5 egg whites in a large bowl. Beat to soft peaks, add cream of tartar, and beat until stiff peaks form, about 2 minutes. Remove the whites to another bowl, and set them aside.

3 Make the batter.

Pour the cake mix, 2 reserved egg yolks, lemon juice, water, and oil into the bowl of your stand mixer. Beat for 30 seconds at low speed to moisten, then beat at high speed for 2 minutes to mix. Fold in the grated lemon zest and beaten egg whites using a couple of turns with the wire whisk.

4 Bake the cake.

Turn the batter into the prepared pan, and bake on the middle rack of the preheated oven until a toothpick inserted into the center comes out clean, about 40 minutes.

5 Make the glaze.

Stir together the confectioners' sugar with enough lemon juice to make a thin mixture.

6 Finish the cake.

Remove the cake from the oven when done, and cool it in the pan on a rack for 10 minutes, or until sides begin to pull away from the pan; then flip it onto a cake plate. Remove the cake pan carefully. Drizzle the warm cake with the glaze, and finish with long curls of lemon zest.

pineapple–macadamia nut cake with four-minute coconut frosting

The most popular cake sold by a certain well-known mail-order cake company, it's still best if you make it at home. And our almost-instant frosting is the twenty-first century's answer to seven-minute frosting. Kids from eight to eighty love this cake. It's a great keeper, too; if stored in a tin, it will be good after a week.

1 tablespoon all-purpose flour

1 (18.5-ounce) package white cake mix, with pudding

¼ cup canola oil

3 large eggs

1 cup crushed pineapple and juice

1 cup freshly squeezed orange juice

1 tablespoon grated orange zest

4-Minute Coconut Frosting

½ cup sugar

2 large egg whites

2 tablespoons water

1 (about 7-ounce) jar marshmallow cream

2 tablespoons shredded coconut

1 tablespoon chopped oil-roasted salted macadamia nuts

makes 16 servings
time: 50 minutes

1 Prepare the pan.

Preheat the oven to 350°F. Spritz a Bundt cake pan with vegetable oil cooking spray. Dust with the flour, coating all surfaces. Turn the pan upside down over a sheet of wax paper, and tap it to remove excess flour. Set it aside.

2 Mix the batter.

Place the cake mix, oil, eggs, pineapple, orange juice, and zest in the bowl of a stand mixer. Mix for 30 seconds on low to moisten; then mix at high speed for 2 minutes. Pour the batter into the prepared pan.

3 Bake the cake.

Bake on the middle rack of the preheated oven until a toothpick inserted into the center comes out clean, about 45 minutes.

4 Make the frosting.

About 5 minutes before removing the cake from the oven, prepare the frosting by placing the sugar, egg whites, and water in a heavy saucepan. Cook over low heat, beating constantly with an electric hand mixer or a wire whisk until soft peaks form, about 3 minutes. Remove the pan from the heat, and add the marshmallow cream. Beat until stiff peaks form, about 2 minutes.

5 Finish the cake.

When the cake is done, remove it to a rack to cool for 10 minutes, or until the cake pulls away from the sides. Turn the cake out onto a paper-doily-lined, footed cake stand. Use a spatula to scoop frosting onto the cake. Once you have it covered, dust the top with the coconut and chopped macadamia nuts.

cinnamon-apple pound cake
with a cider sauce

Yes. This is one of those cakes that makes your house smell like a home. It's heaven. And it's easy.

makes 16 servings
time: 50 minutes

- ¼ cup sugar
- 1 tablespoon plus 2 teaspoons ground cinnamon
- 1 (18.5-ounce) package yellow cake mix with pudding
- ¼ cup sweetened condensed milk
- 4 large egg whites
- 5 tablespoons unsweetened applesauce
- 1¼ cup buttermilk

Cider Sauce

- 1 cup apple cider or juice
- ⅓ cup packed brown sugar
- ⅓ cup butter
- 1 teaspoon cinnamon

1 Prepare the pan.

Preheat the oven to 350°F. Spritz a Bundt cake pan with cooking spray. Mix the sugar and 2 teaspoons cinnamon, and dust the pan to coat all sides with the mixture.

2 Mix the batter.

In the bowl of a stand mixer, combine the cake mix, 1 tablespoon cinnamon, condensed milk, egg whites, applesauce, and buttermilk. Mix on low for 30 seconds to moisten; then mix well for 2 minutes. Pour into the prepared pan.

3 Bake the cake.

Place the pan on the middle rack of the oven until golden or until a toothpick inserted into the center comes out clean, 40 to 45 minutes.

4 Make the sauce.

Combine the apple cider, brown sugar, butter, and cinnamon in a small saucepan. Boil slowly until it is reduced by half.

5 Serve.

Remove the cake from the oven, and let it stand on a rack in the cake pan for 10 minutes; then invert onto a footed cake plate. Drizzle warm sauce over the top, and serve the remainder in a small pitcher on the side.

butter-pecan rum-soaked sheet cake

Poke holes in a warm cake and soak it with a flavorful sauce and you have a cake that tastes great, keeps like a charm and makes a great take-along for a party.

1 tablespoon flour

1 (18.25-ounce) package yellow cake mix with pudding

1 cup water

½ cup rum, 80 proof

3 large egg whites

¼ cup canola oil

Butter-Pecan Rum Glaze

2 tablespoons butter

1 cup brown sugar, packed

1 tablespoon chopped pecans

¼ cup rum, 80 proof

makes 16 servings
time: 50 minutes

1 Prepare the pan.

Preheat the oven to 350°F. Spritz a 9 × 13-inch glass utility pan with cooking spray; then dust it with the flour. Turn the pan upside down to tap out any excess flour. Set aside.

2 Mix the batter.

Place the cake mix, water, rum, egg whites, and oil into the bowl of a stand mixer. Mix for 30 seconds on low to moisten; then mix at high speed for 2 minutes. Pour the batter into the prepared pan.

3 Bake the cake.

Place the pan on the middle rack of the preheated oven, and bake until a toothpick inserted into the center comes out clean, 25 to 35 minutes.

4 Make the glaze.

Meanwhile, prepare the Butter Pecan Rum Glaze by combining the butter, sugar, pecans, and rum in a small saucepan. Boil until the sugar is dissolved and the mixture reduces by one third, about 10 minutes.

5 Finish the cake.

Poke holes into the top of the hot cake, and pour in the rum mixture. Let it cool; then cut it into 2-inch squares to serve.

berry-spice swirl cake

Use the best berries you can find in season and all-fruit preserves to make a fruity marbled cake with a kick of spice to it.

¼ cup sugar

2 teaspoons cinnamon

2 teaspoons ground ginger

1 teaspoon ground cloves

1 cup all-fruit seedless berry jam (blackberry, raspberry, blueberry, strawberry—your choice)

1 yellow cake mix with pudding (18.25-ounce) package

1 cup buttermilk

3 large eggs

¼ cup butter, softened

2 tablespoons confectioners' sugar

1 cup fresh berries of your choice (for garnish)

makes 16 servings
time: 50 minutes

1 Prepare the pan.

Preheat the oven to 350°F. In a small bowl, combine the sugar with the cinnamon, ginger, and cloves. Spritz a Bundt cake pan with cooking spray; then coat all surfaces with the sugar and spice. Place a sheet of wax paper on the counter, and tap the cake pan, releasing excess sugar and spice mixture. Pour this mixture into a small bowl, and stir it together with the berry jam.

2 Mix the batter.

Place the cake mix, buttermilk, eggs, and soft butter in the bowl of a stand mixer. Mix slowly to moisten, about 30 seconds; then turn to high and beat for 2 minutes. Turn the batter out into the prepared pan, holding back one fourth of the batter. Spoon the berry jam in tablespoonfuls all around the cake. Use a knife to cut the spicy jam mixture into the batter to form a swirl. Top with the remaining cake batter. Smooth the top with a spatula.

3 Bake the cake.

Place the pan on the middle rack of the oven, and bake until a toothpick inserted into the center comes out clean, about 45 minutes.

4 Finish the cake.

Cool in the pan on a rack for 10 minutes, or until cake pulls away from the sides. Turn the cake out onto a paper-doily-lined, footed cake stand. Dust with the powdered sugar. Garnish with the fresh berries.

warm lemon cake

Let it be your secret that this cake starts with a cake mix. Serve it hot or cold—it will wow your guests.

1 (17-ounce) box yellow cake mix plus ingredients as listed on the box

Grated zest and juice of 4 lemons

Glaze

½ to 1 cup powdered sugar

2 tablespoons milk

makes 12 servings
time: 45 minutes

1 Prepare the pan.

Preheat the oven to 350°F. Grease and flour a Bundt pan.

2 Mix the batter.

Follow the directions on the box, except use the lemon juice instead of the quantity of liquid called for. If the lemons yield slightly less liquid, add water to make up the difference. Mix thoroughly, and transfer to the prepared cake pan.

3 Bake the cake.

Place the Bundt pan on the center rack, and cook for 35 minutes, or until a toothpick inserted into the center comes out clean. Remove the cake from the oven and let it sit for about 5 minutes. Remove the cake from the pan, and sprinkle it with the powdered sugar.

4 Make the glaze.

Mix powdered sugar and milk. Drizzle it on the cooled cake, and let it run down the sides. This cake can be made a day in advance and cooled in the refrigerator, if you wish.

5 Finish the cake.

You may either serve the cake warm, toast it to rewarm it, or serve it cool. Just sprinkle more powdered sugar on top, and go.

chocolate-bourbon bundt cake

Germans put sauerkraut in everything. Adding kraut to a chocolate cake mix lifts it to a new place. Think of it as having the same principle as carrot cake: great texture, heightened flavor. Plus, soaking a cake in spirits not only makes it taste good, but makes it keep much longer. Dust it with powdered sugar if you wish for a black-and-white finish. This cake is black, bittersweet, and rich.

1 (18.25-ounce) chocolate cake mix, with pudding	*makes 16 servings*
1 tablespoon all-purpose flour	*time: 50 minutes*

1 (18.25-ounce) chocolate cake mix, with pudding

1 tablespoon all-purpose flour

1 tablespoon Dutch-process cocoa

½ cup rinsed, drained, and chopped sauerkraut

4 large egg whites

1¼ cups buttermilk (from skim milk)

¼ cup fat-free sweetened condensed milk

⅓ cup water

Chocolate-Bourbon Soak

¼ cup water

⅓ cup sugar

1 teaspoon Dutch-process cocoa

2 tablespoons unsalted butter

½ cup bourbon

1 Prepare the pan.

Preheat the oven to 350°F. Spritz a 10-inch Bundt pan with cooking spray.

2 Mix the batter.

In a mixing bowl, combine the cake mix, flour, and cocoa. Stir to mix. Add the sauerkraut, and stir to mix. Add the egg whites, buttermilk, sweetened condensed milk, and water. Beat for 3 minutes at medium speed. Pour the batter into the prepared pan.

3 Bake the cake.

Place the pan on the middle rack of the oven, and bake until a toothpick inserted into the center comes out clean, about 50 minutes.

4 Make the chocolate-bourbon soak.

Combine the water, sugar, cocoa, and butter in a small saucepan. Bring to a boil, and dissolve the sugar. Add bourbon.

5 Finish the cake.

Cool the cake in the pan on a rack for about 5 minutes, or until cake begins to pull away from the sides. Flip it over onto a cake serving dish. Pour the chocolate bourbon soak over it slowly. Cool completely before covering the cake with a clear glass cake bell.

tropical torte with coconut, pineapple, and pistachio nuts

Make four thin layers, and the cake not only cooks up quicker, but also develops a luscious caramelized flavor. Whip up the frosting while the cake bakes, and it goes together in a flash. The pineapple makes it keep well. The coconut and pistachios make it pretty.

1 tablespoon all-purpose flour

1 (14-ounce) banana quick bread and muffin mix

1/2 cup buttermilk

1 (8-ounce) can crushed pineapple in unsweetened pineapple juice

2 tablespoons canola oil

1/2 cup mashed ripe banana

3 tablespoons rum (or water, plus 1/2 teaspoon rum extract)

1 teaspoon vanilla extract

2 large eggs

1/2 cup finely chopped pistachios

Frosting

1/2 cup sugar

2 tablespoons water

2 large egg whites

1 jar (7 ounces or 1 1/2 cups) marshmallow cream

1/2 cup angel flake coconut

makes 12 servings
time: 1 hour

1 Prepare the pans.

Preheat the oven to 400°F. Spritz 4 (8-inch) cake pans with cooking spray, and dust with flour, shaking out the excess.

2 Make the batter.

Place the mix, buttermilk, 1/2 cup of the crushed pineapple, oil, banana, rum, vanilla, and eggs in a large bowl. Stir about 50 strokes with a large wooden spoon, until all ingredients are moistened. Fold in the nuts.

3 Bake the cakes.

Divide the batter evenly among the pans. Bake until the tops are golden brown, about 20 minutes. Remove them to a rack. Cool in the pans for 3 minutes, then flip out onto racks, and cool for 10 minutes.

4 Make the frosting.

While the cakes are baking, make the frosting. In a medium saucepan, combine the sugar, water, and egg whites. Whisk over medium heat until soft peaks form, about 3 minutes. Turn off the heat, and stir in marshmallow cream. Whip with an electric mixer until peaks form.

5 Finish the cake.

Place one layer on a cake plate. Spread one quarter of the frosting on top. Drizzle one quarter of remaining pineapple and the coconut on top. Repeat until you have frosted all layers.

meredith pollak's rum cake

When Christmas comes around, Meredith makes these yellow cakes with rum in sheet-cake pans for her daughter's school, in little loaf pans and mini-Bundts for friends and neighbors. And now, in her Houston neighborhood, Christmas just isn't Christmas unless her friends get one of her adorable little rum-soaked cakes.

makes 12 servings
time: 50 minutes

- 1 tablespoon all-purpose flour
- 1 (18.25-ounce) package yellow cake mix, with pudding
- 1 cup water
- ½ cup rum (Myers's is the best)
- 4 large eggs
- ½ cup oil
- 1 cup chopped pecans

Rum Glaze

- ¼ pound (1 stick) butter
- 1 cup sugar
- ¼ cup water
- ¼ cup rum

1 Prepare the pan.
Preheat the oven to 350°F. Grease a 13 × 9-inch pan and dust with flour.

2 Mix the batter.
Combine in a mixing bowl the cake mix, water, rum, eggs, and oil. Beat at medium speed for 3 minutes or 450 strokes by hand.

3 Bake the cake.
Sprinkle pecans in the bottom of the prepared pan. Turn out the batter into the pan, and bake until a toothpick inserted into the center comes out clean, about 45 minutes.

4 Make the glaze.
Combine all the glaze ingredients in a microwave-safe glass measure, and microwave until the butter melts and the sugar dissolves.

5 Finish the cake.
Pour the rum glaze over the hot cake directly in the pan. Serve warm.

banana-nut bundt cake

Yes, this takes a while to bake, but you don't have to supervise it, and you'll have sixteen servings of the fastest cake you ever tried, moist, flavorful and all made in one bowl. You didn't even need a cake mix. Only biscuit mix.

1 tablespoon all-purpose flour

1 cup sugar

1 (8-ounce) package whipped cream cheese

1 cup ripe mashed banana

3 large eggs

2 cups packaged biscuit mix

½ cup chopped walnuts

Confectioners' sugar

makes 16 servings
time: 1 hour

1 Prepare the pan.

Preheat the oven to 350°F. Spritz a 10-inch Bundt pan with cooking spray. Dust it with flour, knocking out the excess.

2 Make the batter.

In a large bowl, using an electric mixer, whip the sugar and cream cheese until fluffy; then whip in the banana and eggs until light and well blended. Stir in the biscuit mix, and beat with a wooden spoon for about 50 strokes, or just until well blended. Fold in the nuts. Pour the batter into the prepared pan.

3 Bake the cake.

Bake on the middle rack of the oven until a toothpick inserted into the center comes out clean and the cake is done, 40 to 55 minutes. Cool on a rack for about 5 minutes; then turn the cake out onto a cake plate.

4 Serve.

Dust the top with powdered sugar sifted through a strainer, and cut the cake into slices.

chapter eight *
enchanting desserts
you can whip up in a flash

What can you make that offers instant relief from the attack of the sugar monster? Starting with cakes from the bakery, fresh fruit, ready-made dessert sauces, liqueurs, and nuts, in moments you can be eating sweet simplicity.

1. Vin Santo Ice Cream with Toasted Walnuts

2. Chocolate Fondue

3. Mini Phyllo Dough Shells Filled with Brummell and Brown Creamy Fruit Spread

4. Lime Jelly Thumbprint Cookies

5. Deep Dish Crumble Top Berry Pie

6. Swiss Cheese and Fruit Tart

vin santo ice cream with toasted walnuts

Want to fool the guests? Stir this together in your ice-cream maker. No one will ever guess you began with store-bought vanilla. Can't find Italy's fabulous dessert wine, Vin Santo? Use marsala instead.

1 pint softened Häagen-Dazs vanilla ice cream

½ teaspoon cinnamon

¼ cup chopped toasted walnuts*

¼ cup Vin Santo (or marsala)

makes 6 servings
time: 10 minutes, plus freezing time

Make the dessert.

Stir all the ingredients together, and place in the freezer for at least 30 minutes before serving. Serve in balloon wineglasses.

---

* To toast walnuts, place them in a dry skillet over high heat, and cook and stir until they begin to color up and have a toasty aroma, about 3 minutes. Whisk the nuts off the fire, and transfer them to a bowl to cool.

chocolate fondue

A communal dessert ends a gathering on just the right note. Pull up your chairs. Pass around the forks. Stick your nose in the fondue pot. The intoxicating aroma of chocolate will charm everyone who is lucky enough to be invited to gather at your table.

8 ounces best quality bittersweet chocolate ice cream sauce (not unsweetened)

½ cup whipping cream

2 teaspoons (packed) orange zest

3 tablespoons Grand Marnier or triple sec*

Angel food cake, cut into 2-inch cubes (substitute pound cake if you wish)

8 strawberries

8 orange sections

8 apple sections

8 banana sections

8 pineapple slices

Any fruit that you especially like

makes 4 servings
time: 5 minutes

1 Melt the chocolate sauce.

In a large bowl, melt the chocolate sauce in the microwave on HIGH (100 percent power) for 3 minutes, or until barely melted.

2 Thin and season the sauce.

Stir in the cream, orange zest, and Grand Marnier.

3 Serve.

Transfer the sauce to fondue pot, and place over a heat source. Serve with the cake pieces and fruit for dipping.

* May substitute brandy, Kahlúa, Cassis, marsala, or kirsch.

mini phyllo dough shells
filled with brummell and brown creamy fruit spread

Brummell and Brown cream is another one of our great discoveries with this book. A by-product of yogurt, this spread designed for bagels is delicious for quick desserts. Here we call for berries, one of the earth's great convenience foods. They're beautiful and come ready to go—no slicing necessary. Just wash them and eat.

1 (15-shell) package mini phyllo shells

30 teaspoons (about ½ cup) Brummell and Brown cream, simply strawberry flavor

1½ cups fresh or frozen raspberries, blueberries, or some of each

makes 4 to 5 servings
time: 15 minutes

1 Preheat the oven to 350° F.

2 Cook the shells.
Place the shells on a cookie sheet, and bake on the center rack of the oven. Cook for 3 minutes, until the edges begin to brown. Let them cool for 5 minutes.

3 Fill the shells.
Fill each shell with 2 teaspoons of Brummell cream and about three berries. Refrigerate until serving time. Can be made up several hours in advance.

lime jelly thumbprint cookies

There are so many unique jellies on the market today that this cookie can be very interesting. Here we use Rose's lime marmalade. This recipe is a great rainy day project for kids.

1 (18-ounce tube) sugar cookie dough
½ heaping cup lime marmalade such as Rose's

makes 4 servings
time: 20 minutes

1 **Preheat oven to 350°F.**

2 **Make the cookies.**
Roll the dough into 1½-inch-diameter balls, and using your thumb, make a shallow indentation. Fill each thumbprint with ¼ teaspoon of marmalade.

3 **Bake the cookies.**
Place the cookie sheets on the center rack of the oven, and bake for 10 to 12 minutes, until the edges begin to brown. Store the cookies in an airtight container.

note: You can use any variety of jelly, lemon or raspberry curd, even caramel sauce.

deep dish crumble top
berry pie

Frozen berries, stashed in the freezer, get you halfway to a quick and homey dessert. If, perchance, you snatched up a pint of fresh berries, you certainly can throw them into this easy pie. There's no crust at all to this pie, except the topping, so don't get yourself in a lather over making piecrust either. No need.

Pie Filling

makes 8 servings
time: 45 minutes

- ½ cup packed brown sugar
- ½ cup granulated sugar
- ¼ teaspoon freshly grated nutmeg
- 1 teaspoon ground cinnamon
- ¼ teaspoon salt
- 3 tablespoons all-purpose flour
- 2 cups frozen berries of your choice
- Juice and zest of ½ lemon

Crumble Crust

- ¼ cup packed brown sugar
- ¼ cup granulated sugar
- ¾ cup all-purpose flour
- ¼ cup rolled oats
- 4 tablespoons (½ stick) butter, softened

Whipped cream

1 Prepare the pan.
Preheat the oven to 350°F. Spritz a deep dish 3-quart casserole with cooking spray.

2 Mix the dry ingredients.
Place the sugars, nutmeg, cinnamon, salt, and flour in a small bowl, and toss to mix.

3 Make the filling.
Arrange the berries in the baking dish. Pour the lemon juice and zest over, and toss to mix. Stir in the sugar mixture, and toss to mix.

4 Make the crumble crust.

Stir together in the same bowl the sugars, flour, and oatmeal. Add the butter, and rub the dry ingredients into butter to form a mixture that resembles coarse crumbs. Sprinkle the crumbs over the top of the berries.

5 Bake the pie.

Place the pan on the center rack, and bake until the crumble top browns, about 45 minutes.

6 Serve.

Spoon the pie into a dessert dish, and pass the cream.

swiss cheese and fruit tart

Who knew cookie dough from a tube could produce such an intriguing dessert?
Don't tell the secret of this fast tart. No rolling pin necessary.

1 cup (3 to 4 ounces) Swiss cheese, shredded

1 (1-pound) tube sugar cookie dough

1 cup shredded coconut

¾ cup currant or other red seedless jelly or apricot jelly

2 tablespoons cassis, brandy, or fruit liqueur

2 cups fruit* of the season (apples, grape halves, kiwi), sliced

makes 6 to 8 servings
time: 25 minutes

1 Prepare the pan.
Preheat the oven to 375°F. Spritz a tart pan with vegetable oil cooking spray.

2 Make the tart shell.
Knead the cheese into the dough slightly, and spread the dough by hand into a 12-inch tart pan, smoothing with your hands and creating a slight lip around the edge. Bake for 10 minutes; then remove the shell from the oven, and sprinkle it evenly with the coconut. Continue baking for 15 minutes, or until the crust is lightly browned. Remove from oven, and mash down using a clean cloth.

3 Make the glaze.
While the crust is baking, whisk the jelly and liqueur together in a medium glass bowl. Cook in the microwave on HIGH (100 percent power). Melt the glaze for 2 minutes. Remove from the microwave, and whisk again.

4 Top the tart.
Arrange the fruit in an attractive pattern on the crust while it's still warm. Drizzle the glaze over the top of the tart. Cut into thin wedges to serve. Good both warm and cold.

✳ Other fruit combos to use all year long include: Nectarines, raspberries, and blueberries for summer. Apples, cranberries, and dates in autumn. Mangoes, pineapple, and papayas in winter. Strawberries and cooked rhubarb in spring.

dessert sauces

Available year-round, frozen fruit should be a constant in everyone's freezer. Though it won't have the texture of fresh fruit, frozen fruit can actually have more flavor than fresh fruit because it is frozen at the peak of its individual season. Here are three recipes done "in minutes" that will leave diners weak in the knees.

1. **Warm Strawberry Red Wine Vinegar Sauce**

2. **Raspberries Macerated in Balsamic Vinegar**

3. **Peaches Macerated in Marsala Wine**

warm strawberry red wine vinegar sauce

This complex flavored strawberry sauce adds a special zing to ice cream or purchased pound cake. For a real audience pleaser, try placing toasted pound cake and a scoop of ice cream in a pool of this wonderful sauce. Outstanding!

1 (¾-pound) bag frozen strawberries

¼ cup sugar

2 tablespoons red wine vinegar

makes 6 to 8 servings
time: 10 minutes

1 Thaw strawberries.
Place the strawberries in a large glass or ceramic bowl, and microwave on HIGH (100 percent power) for 5 minutes.

2 Drain the strawberries.
Transfer the thawed strawberries to a colander, and drain them thoroughly. Return them to the bowl.

3 Finish the sauce.
Stir in the sugar and vinegar, and microwave on HIGH for 3 to 5 minutes, uncovered, until the sauce is boiling. This sauce may be rewarmed, served at once, or served cold.

raspberries macerated in balsamic vinegar

Pucker your lips—this sauce is wonderful on ice cream or angel food cake. You could even use it to spoon over a frozen or purchased cheesecake.

1 (³/₄-pound) bag frozen raspberries

¼ cup sugar

2 tablespoons balsamic vinegar

makes 6 to 8 servings
time: 10 minutes

1 Thaw the raspberries.
Place the raspberries in a large glass or ceramic bowl, and microwave on HIGH (100 percent power) for 5 minutes.

2 Drain the raspberries.
Transfer the thawed raspberries to a colander, and drain thoroughly. Return them to the bowl.

3 Finish the sauce.
Stir in the sugar and balsamic vinegar, and microwave on HIGH for 3 to 5 minutes, uncovered, until the sauce is boiling. The sauce may be rewarmed, served at once, or served cold.

peaches macerated in marsala wine

You don't have to wait for that evanescent peach harvest. Choose frozen peaches that were picked and frozen at their best, then add Marsala. It's summer no matter what time of year.

1 (¾-pound) bag frozen peaches
½ cup sugar
¾ cup marsala

makes 6 to 8 servings
time: 15 minutes

1 Thaw the peaches.
Place the frozen peaches in a large glass or ceramic bowl, and microwave on HIGH (100 percent power) for 10 minutes.

2 Drain the peaches.
Transfer the thawed peaches to a colander, and drain them thoroughly. Return them to the bowl.

3 Cook the peaches.
Stir in the sugar, and cook on HIGH for 7 minutes longer uncovered, until the sauce is boiling.

4 Finish the sauce.
Stir in the marsala, and cook on HIGH for 1 minute longer. The sauce may be rewarmed, served at once, or served cold.

index